Frontiers in Economic History

Series Editors

Claude Diebolt, Faculty of Economics, BETA, CNRS, University of Strasbourg, Strasbourg, France

Michael Haupert, University of Wisconsin–La Crosse, La Crosse, USA

Economic historians have contributed to the development of economics in a variety of ways, combining theory with quantitative methods, constructing new databases, promoting interdisciplinary approaches to historical topics, and using history as a lens to examine the long-term development of the economy. Frontiers in Economic History publishes manuscripts that push the frontiers of research in economic history in order to better explain past economic experiences and to understand how, why and when economic change occurs. Books in this series will highlight the value of economic history in shedding light on the ways in which economic factors influence growth as well as social and political developments. This series aims to establish a new standard of quality in the field while offering a global discussion forum toward a unified approach in the social sciences.

Roger L. Ransom · Jared David McKenzie

Imperial Wars in the Modern Era

The Struggling for Territory

Springer

Roger L. Ransom
Department of History
University of California, Riverside
Riverside, CA, USA

Jared David McKenzie
Riverside, CA, USA

ISSN 2662-9771 ISSN 2662-978X (electronic)
Frontiers in Economic History
ISBN 978-3-032-07700-4 ISBN 978-3-032-07701-1 (eBook)
https://doi.org/10.1007/978-3-032-07701-1

© The Editor(s) (if applicable) and The Author(s), under exclusive license to Springer Nature Switzerland AG 2025

This work is subject to copyright. All rights are solely and exclusively licensed by the Publisher, whether the whole or part of the material is concerned, specifically the rights of translation, reprinting, reuse of illustrations, recitation, broadcasting, reproduction on microfilms or in any other physical way, and transmission or information storage and retrieval, electronic adaptation, computer software, or by similar or dissimilar methodology now known or hereafter developed.
The use of general descriptive names, registered names, trademarks, service marks, etc. in this publication does not imply, even in the absence of a specific statement, that such names are exempt from the relevant protective laws and regulations and therefore free for general use.
The publisher, the authors and the editors are safe to assume that the advice and information in this book are believed to be true and accurate at the date of publication. Neither the publisher nor the authors or the editors give a warranty, expressed or implied, with respect to the material contained herein or for any errors or omissions that may have been made. The publisher remains neutral with regard to jurisdictional claims in published maps and institutional affiliations.

This Springer imprint is published by the registered company Springer Nature Switzerland AG
The registered company address is: Gewerbestrasse 11, 6330 Cham, Switzerland

If disposing of this product, please recycle the paper.

Contents

1	**Introduction**	1
	1.1 Wars, Imperialism, and the Gunpowder Revolution	2
	1.2 Guns, Imperialism, and Imperial Wars	3
	1.3 Imperialism and a World War	4
2	**A New World to Explore**	9
	2.1 The Fall of Constantinople and the Spice Trade	9
	2.2 Christopher Columbus Discovers America	10
	2.3 La Isabella a Spanish Colony in the New World	11
	2.4 The Legacy of Christopher Columbus	12
	2.5 The Magellan Del-Cano Expedition	13
	2.6 The New Trade Routes of Columbus and Magella	14
3	**The Spanish Empire**	17
	3.1 Hernan Cortez and the Fall of the Aztec Empire	17
	3.2 Noche Triste: Cortez Is Trapped in Tenochtitlan	18
	3.3 Escape and the Siege of Tenochtitlan	19
	3.4 Francisco Pizzaro and Diego Almagro	19
	3.5 Pizzaro and Almagro Invade Peru	20
	3.6 Pizzaro and Almagro Fight for Cusco	21
	3.7 The Discovery of Gold in New Spain	22
	3.8 The Spanish Treasure Fleets	24
4	**The Spanish Armada**	27
	4.1 Queen Elizabeth's Secret Plan	27
	4.2 Drake's Voyage Around the World	28
	4.3 The Spanish Armada and the Invasion of England	29
	4.4 The Defeat of the Armada	31
5	**The East India Company and the British Empire**	33
	5.1 Inventing the Joint Stock Company	33

6	**The American Revolution**		37
	6.1 British and French Rivalry in Canada		37
	6.2 The 10 Battles of Saratoga, New York		38
	6.3 Implications of the Battles of Saratoga		39
	6.4 The War of 1812		40
7	**The Napoleonic Wars**		41
	7.1 Napoleon Bonaparte and the French Imperial Empire: 1779–1814		41
	7.2 The French Invasion of Russia		43
8	**The Mexican American War**		45
	8.1 The Louisiana Purchase		45
	8.2 The Indian Removal Act		47
	8.3 Slavery and Annexation		48
	8.4 The Introduction of Slavery to the United States		49
	8.5 The Election of 1840 and William Henry Harrison's Death		49
	8.6 Manifest Destiny and the Election of 1844		50
	8.7 A "Joint Resolution" for Annexation of Texas		51
	8.8 Polk's War		51
	8.9 Polk's Plan for the War		52
	8.10 The Battle of Buena Vista		53
	8.11 The Trteaty of Guadalupe Hidalgo		53
9	**The American Civil War**		57
	9.1 Abraham Lincoln as the Imperialist		57
	9.2 Secession and the Civil War		58
	9.3 Emancipation and the South After the Civil War		59
10	**The Crimean War**		61
	10.1 A Fool's Charge		61
11	**CINC: A Measure of Military Capability**		65
	11.1 War, Economics, and the Gunpowder Revolution		65
12	**Bismark's Wars**		67
	12.1 Otto Von Bismark, the Imperialist		67
	12.2 The Seven Weeks War Between Austria and Prussia		68
	12.3 The Franco-Prussian War: Opening Moves		68
	12.4 The Franco-Prussian War		69
	12.5 A Treaty at Last		70
13	**The Spanish American War**		75
	13.1 The United States Declares War on Spain		75
	13.2 The U.S. Senate Ratifies the Treaty of Paris on February 6, 1899.		76

14	**The Russo-Japanese War**		77
	14.1	The Rivalry of Japan and Russia for Manchuria	77
	14.2	The Japanese Attack Russia	77
	14.3	The Battle of Mukden	78
	14.4	Financing the War	78
	14.5	The Battle of Toshima	79
	14.6	The Emergence of Japan as an Imperial Power	80
15	**The Schlieffen Plan**		83
	15.1	World Empires in 1900	83
	15.2	The Schlieffen Plan	83
	15.3	The Assassination of the Archduke Ferdinand	85
	15.4	The Invasion of France in 1914	86
	15.5	The Race to the Sea	87
	15.6	Stalemate on the Western Front	87
16	**The Sideshows: Italy, Gallipoli, and the Middle East**		89
	16.1	The Russian Invasion of East Prussia	89
	16.2	Italy Changes Sides	91
17	**Palestine and Sykes-Picot**		95
	17.1	The Sykes-Picot Agreement	95
18	**The Treaty of Brest-Litovsk**		97
	18.1	Brest-Litovsk	97
	18.2	The United States Enters the War	99
19	**The Ludendorff Offensives**		101
	19.1	Imperialism and Ludendorff's Imperial War	101
	19.2	Operation Michael	101
	19.3	"Operation Georgette"	102
	19.4	"Operation Blucher-Yorck"	102
	19.5	Ludendorff's Results	102
	19.6	The Allies Fight Back	103
	19.7	The Generals Throw in the Towel	104
	19.8	The Collapse of the Central Powers	107
20	**The Treaty of Versailles and the Great Depression**		109
	20.1	Peace for Vultures	109
	20.2	Woodrow Wilson's Fourteen Points	111
	20.3	The Italians and the Japanese Go Home with Their Imperial Appetites Unsated	115
	20.4	Fallout Treaties	116
21	**Adolf Hitler and the Rise of National Socialism**		119
	21.1	Adolf Hitler and the Beer Hall Putsch	119
	21.2	Hitler in Landsberg Prison	119
	21.3	Hitler's Rise to the Head of the Nazi Party	120

22	**Operation Barbarossa**		123
	22.1 A New Age of Warfare		123
	22.2 Josef Stalin and the Soviet Union, 1933–41		123
	22.3 Stuck in Stalingrad		125
	22.4 A Third Reich Collapses		126
23	**Dreams of a Rising Sun**		127
	23.1 A Rising Japan		127
	23.2 Ambitions Burning Too Bright		128
	23.3 Tora, Tora, Tora: The Attack on Pearl Harbor		130
	23.4 The Dolittle Raids		131
	23.5 Battle at the Coral Sea		131
24	**The Battle of Midway**		133
	24.1 The Battle of Midway		133
	24.2 Island Hoping and the DUKW Landing Crafts		134
	24.3 The Manhattan Project and the Trinity Test		135
	24.4 Impact of the Trinity Test		136
25	**Closing**		139
	25.1 The Spanish Empire 300 Years of Imperialism		139
	25.2 The American Exception		140
	25.3 The Scared Imperialists		140
Bibliography			141

Chapter 1
Introduction

1.1 Imperialism is a term that has been applied to a wide variety of situations over a very long period of time. A simple definition is that imperialism refers to a situation where one country or empire attempts to impose economic or political restrictions on another country or Empire. It is easy to find examples of imperialism dating back to the empires of antiquity; however, the term became particularly popular for historians studying situations of imperialism in the years following the end of the Roman Empire. Because examples of imperialism tend to involve the use of military force, instances of imperial domination are frequently associated with what we will call "imperial wars." The combatants in these wars usually found ways to end the fighting, but the outcome seldom produced long-term solutions to the problems that started the war. This book will examine a group of Imperial wars that changed existing boundaries, new states and changed the map of Europe and the rest of the world in the years following the Roman Empire.

In his book *Why Did Europe Conquer the World?* historian Phillip Hoffman points out that by the end of the nineteenth century a handful of European nations—most notably Spain, Portugal, Britain, France, Russia, Netherlands, and Belgium—had at one time or another, used their military and economic power to gain control of 84 percent of the habitable area of the world. Figure 1.1 presents a map that shows Hoffman's estimate of the areas of the World in 1919 which had been controlled at some point in time by a European country and those which had escaped European influence. Areas marked "Controlled" had been under the influence of European imperial power at some point before 1919. Areas marked "Free" had managed to escape any European imperialism before 1919. The area marked "Europe" represents European states that were part of the Roman Empire before the fifteenth century. The only area of the map that had escaped some form of Imperial intervention consisted of the Ottoman Empire and most of China, Japan, and Korea. All the rest had fallen victim to some form of imperial intervention that involved military intervention on the part of some other states.[1]

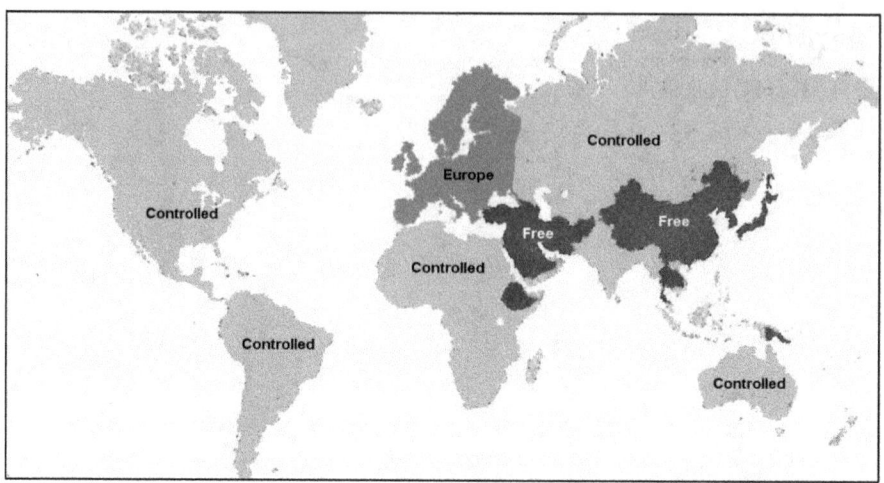

Fig. 1.1 Countries that were controlled by or free from European imperialism, 1450–1914

1.1 Wars, Imperialism, and the Gunpowder Revolution

By the middle of the fifteenth-century warfare among European countries was experiencing a process of dramatic change with the introduction of a wide variety of weapons using gunpowder. Infantry units could be equipped with soldiers carrying weapons that could reach targets several hundred yards away. Cannons in artillery units could destroy walls and fortifications and inflict devastating volleys of "Grapeshot" into the ranks of advancing infantry. European soldiers were strictly governed by rules of movement during a battle, and both infantry and cavalry units wore armor made of tempered steel. The introduction of guns, discipline, and armor had a major effect on the fighting between European armies and the unarmored warriors of societies that lacked gunpowder weapons and steel armor. A very small group of well-armed European soldiers—sometimes as few as several hundred men and a small unit of cavalry—could hold off the undisciplined attacks of hundreds of warriors lacking guns and amor in Africa, Asia, or the Americas.

The gunpowder revolution was extremely expensive and only a small group of European countries could afford to spend the vast share of government resources needed to equip their units with gunpowder weapons. Hoffman postulates several conditions that needed to be present for countries to make use of gunpowder weapons. Countries must be involved with frequent wars in order to justify the substantial expenses of maintaining armies to sustain the new weapons. Rulers must also be willing to use the new weapons even though they were so expensive.

Hoffman points out that these conditions were all met in Early Modern Europe and he leaves little doubt that the use of gunpowder weapons can explain why the European countries were able to conquer 84 percent of the habitable world with their wars. He develops what he calls a Tournament Model of European warfare to explain why European rulers got caught up in endless efforts to win some sort of prizes out of the victories that were obtained in these wars.[2]

1.2 Guns, Imperialism, and Imperial Wars

The "prizes" won in imperial wars from 1450 to 1900 were almost always tied to quarrels over the acquisition of new territories through an imperial war. This book deals with some of the more important "imperial wars" in the period from the fall of Constantinople to the Turkish forces in 1453 to the end of the Second World War in 1945.

The Spanish built an empire that dominated the European spice trade with the Orient for 150 years. By the end of the sixteenth century, they had used small "armies" of professional soldiers armed with steel weapons to conquer and construct an empire that stretched from the tip of South America to the border of the English colony that was the southern border of British Canada. The Spanish imperial wars were conflicts between established soldiers of European armies that had fought each other in Europe against the unarmored troops of less-developed empires in the newly discovered world of North and South America.

By the end of the eighteenth century, imperial wars were being fought in America between two European countries that both had gunpowder weapons. In 1783 Britain's American Colonies won their imperial war against the British Empire, and in the beginning of the nineteenth century Napoleon Bonaparte won a series of battles that allowed him to build a French Empire that stretched from Paris to the western border of Russia. He then got into a dispute with the Czar and invaded Russia. The invasion failed and Bonaparte's imperial effort was defeated by the British and Prussians in the Battle of Waterloo in 1815.

1.3 Imperialism and a World War

By the end of the nineteenth century, the scale of imperial war had escalated to a point where the Russians and the Japanese were fighting each other over Eastern Manchuria and Northern China in the last of what we might call a "limited Imperial war." At this point the major European states started to fight over each others' territories and imperial wars reached a new level of warfare. In 1914 the Germans again invaded France; a move that this time produced a conflict that started a World War.

Most historians do not refer to the First World War as an "imperial" war. However, historian Richard Overy offers a powerful argument that:

> In a very obvious sense the Great War was an imperial war– all the states that joined it in 1914–15 were empires, either traditional dynastic empires or nations with overseas imperial territories. As the war became a prolonged attritional conflict, the stakes were raised so that the very survival of the nation-empire defined the nature of the struggle. Historical focus on the long and sanguinary stalemate on the Western Front has rendered the conflict in narrowly nationalist terms, but the war was fought worldwide and with clear imperial ambitions.[3]

The Treaty of Paris in 1919 ended the fighting for territories in the First World War, but it did not end the European states' appetite for imperial gains. On September 27, 1940, Germany, Japan, and Italy formed the Tripartite Pact, which eventually led to another world war that included a host of imperial sideshows. Our book is not attempting to provide a full historical analysis of wars fought between 1450 and 1945. We deal with what lay behind each of the most important imperial outcomes of fourteen imperial wars, and how the outcome of those wars shaped history.

Table 1.1 describes the major imperial wars discussed in the book.

1.3 Imperialism and a World War

Table 1.1 Imperial conflicts: 1519 1945

Chapter	Conflict	Date	Imperial country	Attacked country	Outcome
3	Hernan Cortez Attacks Aztec Empire	1519–21	Spain	Aztec Empire	Aztec Empire was Destroyed and the Spanish Spanish create the Spanish Empire
3	Francisco Pizzaro and Diego Almagro Invade Inca Empire	1531–71	Spain	Incan Empire	The Inca Empire in Spanish America is Destroyed The Spanish Empire is expanded to include create Peru
5	Francis Drake's Voyage Around The World	1577–80	English	Spain	Drake's Raid circumvents the Globe He Captures Spanish Treasure Establishes English World Naval Power
6	English–Spanish Rivalry	1577–1603	Spain	English	Spanish Armada Plans to Invade England—Armada Fails
8	The American Revolution	1775–83	Britain	American Rebels	American Colonists Rebel Against Great Britain They Gain Freedoms as United States of America
9	Napoleon Bonaparte's French Empire	1803–15	France	Russia	Napoleon Creates French Empire From Paris to Moscow Russians Drive Him out of Russia Napoleon loses the *Battle of Waterloo*
10	Mexican American War	1845–48	United States	Mexico	Mexico is Defeated in war with United States *Treaty of Guadalupe Hidalgo f*orces Mexico to Cede California to United States

(continued)

Table 1.1 (continued)

Chapter	Conflict	Date	Imperial country	Attacked country	Outcome
11	Crimean War	1853–56	Britain France Turkey	Russia	Britain and France Resist Russia's Expansion in the Middle East *The Treaty of Paris* Ends the War
12	American Civil War	1861–65	North United States	South United States	Southern States try to leave Union Northerners Win Civil War *Savery is abolished* in United States
13	Bismark's War	1870–71	Prussia	France	Bismark Starts *Franco-Prussian War* France Loses War and *Cedes Alsace-Lorraine to Germany* Bismark Becomes *German Emperor*
14	Spanish American War	1898	United States	Spain	United States Wins *Spanish American War* and Spain is pushed out of the Philippines by the *United States*
15	Russo-Japanese War	1904–05	Japan	Russia	*Japan* defeats *Russia* in the *Russo-Japanese War* Annexes *East Manchuria and Gains Control of Port Arthur*
16	The Schlieffen Plan	1914	Germany	France/Germany	Germany invades France but is prevented from ever reaching Paris as the growing conflict leads to WWI.

(continued)

Table 1.1 (continued)

Chapter	Conflict	Date	Imperial country	Attacked country	Outcome
22	Operation Barbarossa	1941	Germany	Soviet Union	Inspired by a string of success' the Third Reich invades USSR and involves the Russians in WWII
23	Pearl Habor	1941	Japan	U.S.A.	Japanese drag the United States into WWII and end up losing their hegemony in the Pacific Ocean as a result.

Notes

1. Hoffman explains that areas under control here include Europe itself and former colonies in the Americas and the Russian Empire but not the non European parts of the Ottoman Empire.
   He cites the 84 percent estimate as coming from Headrick (1981, 3) See Hoffman (2015) for a more detailed discussion of the map.
2. Hoffman (2015).
3. Overy (2021, 12).

Chapter 2
A New World to Explore

2.1 The Fall of Constantinople and the Spice Trade

In 1453 the forces of the Ottoman Empire finally succeeded in capturing the city of Constantinople. The Ottoman victory meant that the last vestige of the once powerful Roman Empire was no longer open to free trade by European governments. At a time when the world lacked an effective form of artificial refrigeration, spices such as pepper, cinnamon, nutmeg, clove, ginger, turmeric, and anise were all in great demand throughout Europe to preserve the flavor of perishable food, and some of these spices were thought to be useful in dealing with the effects of a variety of diseases. The spices were primarily grown in a group of islands located in the southern part of the Philippines just west of Guiana that were known as the "Spice Islands." By 1500 a substantial trade had developed between the Spice Islands and European traders. The Europeans did not know the even know the exact location of these islands. They picked up their cargos from suppliers in northern China. From there they followed a variety of routes known as the "Silk Roads," which wound their way through China, Central Asia, and the Ottoman Empire on the way to Constantinople.[1] When the Ottoman Empire captured Constantinople, the silk roads were abruptly closed to Europeans, and they had to look for new routes that might lead them to the Spice Islands. An obvious possibility would be the discovery of a more direct route across the Atlantic Ocean that would replace the Silk Roads. Portuguese explorers, led by Prince Henry the Navigator and Vasco Da Gama, had already explored the Western coast of Africa and sailed around the Cape of Good Hope to reach India, but they still had a long way to go before they reached the Spice Islands. A growing number of explorers had reached the conclusion that the most obvious possibility for finding a shorter trade route to Asia would be to sail directly across the Atlantic Ocean. If, as they believed. the world was round, then one should eventually reach the Western coast of Asia and the Spice Islands. From there, they were confident from what they already knew, that there was a route through the Indian Ocean and the Western coast of Europe.

The problem was that no one knew how big the Pacific Ocean was.

2.2   Christopher Columbus Discovers America

One of the most persistent proponents of a solution to these problems was Christopher Columbus. Columbus had approached several monarchs in the 1470s and 80s, in 1484 he approached King John II of Portugal with a proposal to reach the spice Islands by sailing west from Portugal. The king was intrigued by Columbus's ideas, but his advisors insisted they were impractical because Columbus's estimates of the distance to cross the Atlantic and reach Asia were surely too small. Not to be put off, Columbus took a revised version of his plan to the Spanish Crown and he managed to get an audience with Queen Isabella of Castile and King Ferdinand of Aragon. The queen was convinced that Columbus's ideas were practical, and she agreed to help him finance a fleet of three ships; the *Nina* the *Pinta* and the *Santa Maria;* to sail west in search of the Spice Islands.

So it was that on September 3, 1492, Columbus and his three ships left Spain. They stopped at the Canary Islands long enough to get their ships outfitted for the trip that lay ahead and on September 6th they set sail on their way to the Spice Islands. The Southwest trade winds carried them across the Atlantic Ocean, and early on of the evening of October 12th a lookout excitedly shouted that he had seen some land. The next morning long stretches of land were clearly visible to everyone. Five weeks after they left Spain, Columbus and his crew had found one of the larger Islands in the Bahama Islands just northeast of present-day Cuba, which he promptly named San Salvador.[2]

Convinced that this island must be near the eastern coast of China, Columbus and a small party of Spaniards went ashore. They were warmly greeted by the Arakawa natives on the island, and after visiting with them for several days, Columbus left San Salvador and sailed along the north coast of Cuba searching for gold. He had been pleasantly surprised to find that many of the natives he encountered were wearing jewelry that was made of gold, and he knew that nothing would please Isabella and Ferdinand more than the discovery of gold in this remote part of the world. Columbus's search took him to the northern end of Haiti, where the fleet encountered a major problem. One of his ships—the *Sanat Maria*—ran aground and had to be scuttled. To make things worse, several weeks earlier Columbus had quarreled with Alonzo Pinzon—the captain of the *Pinta*—over which course they should take in their search for gold. It turned out that Columbus was not the only explorer who became obsessed with the prospect of discovering gold. Pinzon had simply decided to sail off in a huff to pursue his own search for gold.

Left with only a single boat, Columbus decided to make the best of a difficult situation. Claiming that the wreck of *Santa Maria* was an omen from the Lord, he declared that the Spaniards must build an outpost on this location. Using materials from the grounded ship, the men built a wooden tower and several other structures to form an outpost which Columbus named *Navidad*. He then managed to convince a group of volunteers to remain at Navidad and look for gold while he returned to Spain to gather more supplies and future colonists.[3] Reinforced by the return of Pinzon—who had returned from his unsuccessful search for gold—the *Nina* and the *Pinta* set sail for the voyage back to Spain on January 16, 1493. The south westerly winds that had carried the ships to the New World made the eastbound trip home considerably more difficult, and the two ships did not reach Spain until March 13th.

Columbus's announcement that he had actually reached some islands off the coast of China by sailing west across the Atlantic Ocean was exciting news. Once he got back to Spain, he was able to convince the Spanish monarchs that his creation of Navidad gave the Spanish Crown rights to new territory. Queen Isabella was so excited that she helped organize an armada of 17 ships and more than a thousand men to undertake a second trip of exploration. She hoped that this armada would be enough for Columbus to establish a colony that would mark the beginning of the Spanish trade Empire in the orient. Columbus left on a second voyage to the New World on September 25, 1493.

2.3 La Isabella a Spanish Colony in the New World

Columbus's return to America was not cause for celebration. While he was gone, Navidad had been destroyed by the American natives and the men he left behind had all been killed or were missing. With the much larger contingent of ships and men that he brought with his second trip, Columbus decided that the Spaniards would be able to establish a larger village further along on the southern coast of Cuba and he named of the new village *La Isabella* in honor of the Spanish Queen.

Columbus stayed in the Bahamas for two years as governor of La Isabella. However, this was not a task that he was well suited for. He turned the duties of running the government over to his two brothers, Bartholomew and Christopher so that he could spend most of his time exploring the southern coast of Cuba in an unsuccessful search for gold. While he was away from the town, there was an uproar over arbitrary decisions made by his brothers. Furthermore, the colony had become desperately short of supplies from the home country. Throwing caution to the winds, Columbus decided to once again leave the government of La Isabella in the hands of his brothers while he returned to Spain to get supplies to support the colony.

Isabella and Ferdinand were impressed that Columbus had managed to establish a Spanish colony in the New World, and they were even more impressed by the huge pile of trinkets made of gold that Columbus brought back as evidence that there was gold in the New World. Although they were preoccupied with a war with France at this point, the Queen helped Columbus organize a fleet of six ships filled with supplies for the colonies and she promoted him to "Admiral of the fleet." On May 30, 1498, Columbus left Spain for his third trip across the Atlantic.

He arrived at La Isabella early in July to discover once again that things had not gone well while he was away. The brothers made arbitrary decisions; they were quick to impose heavy penalties on those who disagreed with them, accepted bribes, and the natives were quick to point out that they had been badly treated while Columbus was gone. Soon after he got back from Spain, the situation had reached a point where reports of a revolt against Columbus by Franciso Roldan, one of the prominent Isabella colonists, had reached King Ferdinand. The king decided that he needed to appoint someone to look into the situation, and he appointed Francisco de Bodadilla as a judge with orders to investigate the situation in La Isabella. Bodadilla arrived in La Isabella along with a contingent of 500 soldiers in August of 1500. He carried with him instructions from the king to put things in order and he wasted no time before looking into the accusations against Columbus and his brothers. He found that they had indeed greatly exceeded his authority as governors on many occasions, and he ordered Columbus and his brother Bartholomew be arrested and sent back to Spain in chains.

Once he was back home, Columbus was able to successfully challenge Bodadilla's judgment against him, and he manage to wrangle support for a fourth trip back to America in May of 1502. The King's instructions this time were that Columbus was to find a water route to the orient. Columbus sailed directly to Jamaica and then sailed slowly along the eastern coast of the Isthmus of Panama. Though he went ashore several times, Columbus did not explore the interior of the isthmus and therefore he did not discover that there was an ocean only a few miles from where he was standing. By this time Columbus was encountering major problems with his health, and he returned to Spain in 1504. He died in 1506 still believing that he had reached the outskirts of Asia in his travels.

2.4 The Legacy of Christopher Columbus

Columbus did not find a route to Asia, nor did he find the gold deposits that he was constantly searching for. Because he did not explore the interior of Isthmus of Panama he did not realize how close he came to discovering the Pacific Ocean. It was not until 1513 that a Spanish explorer, Vasco de Balboa, crossed the Isthmus and became the first European in America to view the Pacific Ocean. Nevertheless, Christopher Columbus's voyages had a profound impact on the world after 1500. We will leave it for his esteemed biographer Samuel Eliot Morison to sum up where Columbus stands in the history of the Western world:

> The whole history of the Americas stems from the four voyages of Columbus, and as the Greek city states look back to the deathless God of their founders, so today the score of independent nations and dominions to unite in homage to Christopher, the stout powered son of Genoa who carried Christian civilization across the ocean sea. (Morison 1942).

What Columbus had demonstrated is that if you follow the trade winds going west across the Atlantic Ocean, you would almost surely find a route that would lead you to the Orient. A few years later Vasco de Balboa showed that there was indeed another ocean on the west side of the Isthmus of Panama. To the South of Spanish settlements in Central America the Portuguese were exploring the east coast of South America.

To the North King Henry VII of England was exploring supporting John Cabot's efforts to explore the coast of what would one day become the English colonies in North America. All that remained was to find a water route to the Spice Islands.

2.5 The Magellan Del-Cano Expedition

In September of 1518 King Charles I of Spain responded to this outburst of interest in exploration by funding an expedition to see if it was possible to sail around the world. A growing group of people by this time believed that such a trip would be possible. The king chose Ferdinand Magellan, a Portuguese explorer with experience sailing in the Atlantic Ocean and the coast of South America, to command a small armada of ships that would try to sail around the world.

Magellan left Spain on September 20, 1519, with five ships and 270 men. His fleet stopped at the Canary Islands for provisions and then headed on a Southwest trip across the Atlantic Ocean until they reached the northern coast of Brazil. They then sailed south along the East Brazilian coast; making frequent stops while searching for a passage that would allow them to sail west towards the Spice Islands. They finally reached the southern tip of South America and at this point they discovered a bay that took them to a turbulent strait which provided access to the Pacific Ocean.

After a torturous trip through the strait that would one day bear his name, Magellan had finally found a route to the Pacific Ocean. However, his trip along the Brazilian coast had taken him much further south along the coast of South America than he anticipated before he finally found a water passage to the orient. Moreover, one of his captains, Juan de Cartagena, had become so disoriented while trying to navigate his way through the Strait of Magellan that he eventually turned back to Spain. Magellan was therefore left with only three ships to continue his voyage. Cartagena arrived back in Spain in May of 1521 with news that Magellan had discovered an Ocean on the west side of Panama which would surely offer a way to reach the Orient. But there was no news from Magellan himself.

One of the problems that plagued the explorers seeking a direct sea route to the orient was that they did not have any maps that could guide them across the Pacific Ocean. Magellan anticipated that the trip from the Strait he had found to the Spice Islands would take a few weeks at most. In fact, it took the little fleet three months and twenty days. To further complicate matters, Magellan experienced a sudden burst of religious enthusiasm that led him to try to convert natives of the Philippine Islands to Christianity. He was having some success with this effort as he went from island to island, however the ruler of the island of Mactan was stubbornly resisting his efforts. On April 27 Magellan and members of his crew tried to subdue the Mactans by force. Unfortunately, Magellan was killed in the ensuing battle.

Magellan's death was a blow to the remaining crew members, however they managed to regroup and elect Juan Sebastian El Canon, who had served as the fleet's navigator of the trip on their way to the Philippines, to be the new leader of the expedition. El Cano's first challenge was the loss of another of their ships which was found to be unseaworthy. All of the crew members from the damaged ship got on *Victoria*, which had been Magellan's flagship. El Cano was determined to get *Victoria* and what remained of the crew back to Spain. He successfully guided them through the Indian Ocean; around the Cape of Good Hope at the tip of Africa; and north along the West Coast of Africa to Spain. On September 6, 1522, *Victoria* and 18 of the 270 crew members who had begun Magellan's voyage three years earlier, finally reached home when they arrived at Sanlucar de Barrameda, Spain.

2.6 The New Trade Routes of Columbus and Magella

Figure 2.1 shows the way in which the voyages of Columbus, Magellan, and El Cano opened up new routes between Europe and the spice Islands at the middle of the sixteenth century. The Silk Roads were a set of land and water roots stretching from eastern China to Constantinople that had been closed to Western European traffic by the Ottoman occupation of Constantinople in 1453. The Magellan/El Cano Project proved that it was possible for a boat to sail around the world. This was exciting news to cartographers, but the routes followed by Magellan and El Cano would not be of much value to commercial shippers.[4]

It was Columbus's discovery of a narrow strip of land that lies between the Atlantic and Pacific Oceans that eventually provided a way for Spanish merchants to find a way to get to the orient that dramatically reduced the time and cost of shipping goods between Seville, Spain, and Manilla in the Philippines. They could send their cargoes on ships that would leave Seville and sail across the Atlantic Ocean to the Isthmus of Panama. Mule trains could carry the goods across the Isthmus to the Pacific Ocean, and from there ships could sail across the Pacific Ocean to unload the goods in Manilla and the Spice Islands for a fraction of the cost only a few years earlier.

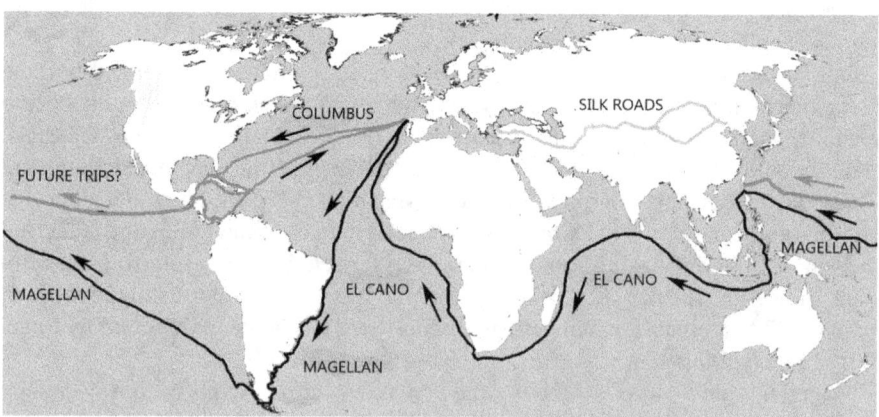

Fig. 2.1 Voyages of Columbus and voyages of Magellan/Cano. *Sources* Bergreen (2003), Cameron (1973), McKee (2018), Morison (1942) and Thomas (2005)

Notes

1. For more on the demand for spices and the evolution of the Silk Roads as a route between Europe and the Orient, see Frankopan (2017) and Crowely (2024).
2. Columbus chose names for many of the places he encountered in the Bahamas. To simplify our discussion, we will use the current names for the geography of the Americas to locate his discoveries.
3. It is unclear how many people Columbus left behind at Navidad while he returned to Spain. Morison (1942) reports 39 men; McKee (2018) reports 36. Both writers stress the lure of finding gold as a major incentive for those who agreed to remain behind.
4. There is a large literature dealing with Magellan's trip around the world. One of the best overall views of the complete voyage is Bergreen (2003). See also Cameron (1973).

Chapter 3
The Spanish Empire

3.1 Hernan Cortez and the Fall of the Aztec Empire

Amid all the hustle and bustle of international trading markets at the beginning of the sixteenth century, the Spanish community in the Americas was rapidly expanding. In the fall of 1518, Hernan Cortez, who was mayor of Havana, managed to fund an expedition to explore the Mexican mainland. Cortez's force consisted of six ships, 350 infantrymen—most of whom were veterans of the Spanish wars in central Europe— 16 horses, 50 sailors, and 14 pieces of artillery of various sizes.[1] With this small but well-armored force, Cortez set forth to conquer the indigenous populations of central Mexico. They landed on the East Coast of the Yucatan Peninsula in February of 1519. After some minor victories over Native Americans, Cortez claimed the region for the Spanish Crown. He then proceeded to take over the town of Veracruz and break his relationship with the Spanish officials in Cuba, who were becoming skeptical of his activities. To prevent any thoughts of returning to Panama, Cortez burned the ships that had brought him to the mainland. The major obstacle confronting him at this point were was the Aztec Empire, whose capital city, Tenochtitlan, was about 350 miles to the west. The city was reported to have a population of more than 200,000 people and it was located in the middle of Lake Texcoco.[2]

On August 8, 1519, Cortez and his men began an extended march to capture the Emperor Montezuma and destroy the Aztec Empire which controlled central Mexico. En route they made stops to secure the support of native groups who disliked the Aztecs. The largest stop was a 20 day visit at the city of Tlaxcala, which was home of a tribe of Native Americans, the Tlaxcalans who were particularly opposed to the rule of the Aztecs, and who became firm allies of the Spaniards adding much needed manpower to Cortez's force. Cortez and his men finally reached Tenochtitlan, accompanied by a large force of Mexican allies, on November 8, 1519—almost a year after they had left Cuba. They were received by the Emperor Montezuma, who was not sure what to make of his visitors. He cautiously invited Cortez and his men to come into the city. Against the strong advice of his allies who warned him that

Montezuma would try to take them all captive, Cortez and his men accepted the emperor's invitation, and they entered the city.

3.2 Noche Triste: Cortez Is Trapped in Tenochtitlan

The advice given to Cortez by his allies was right. Montezuma expected that the Aztec warriors would be able to trap the Spaniards in the narrow streets of Tenochtitlan, which could easily be blocked once the enemy was inside the city. Numerous Aztec warriors could then attack small group of Spaniards from the roofs of buildings. Since the city was completely surrounded by Lake Texcoco, and all of the bridges leading out of the city could be torn down or blocked, the Spaniards would have no place to hide.

Cortez and his men had no intention of hiding. He turned his troops lose to search for every form of gold artifact that could be found and confiscated within the city, and every Spanish soldier would be able to keep a share of what he collected. To protect his troops from interference by Aztecs while his men rampaged throughout the city, Cortez had imprisoned Montezuma as a hostage. However, on June 1st the Aztec Emperor was murdered by a crowd throwing stones. It remains unclear whether the murder was carried out by Aztec soldiers who were angry at their emperor's surrender, or by angry Spanish soldiers searching for gold. Whichever side was to blame for the emperor's murder, it was becoming increasingly clear that the Spanish soldiers had indeed been caught in a trap. Recognizing his dilemma, Cortez ordered his soldiers to build some temporary wooden bridges that would help them deal with the many canals in the city, and they collected 8 tons of gold that the Army had during their rampage through the city. On June 30, 1520, the Spanish made their move to escape. Each man had to decide how much gold to take with him during the escape. For those who chose to keep most of their riches, the weight of the gold combined with the weight of their armor meant that many of them drowned in their attempt to cross the lake. Cortez managed to escape; however, he lost at least half of his command and most of the stolen gold did not make it to the far shore of the lake. What became known as *Noche Triste* was an unmitigated disaster for the Spanish. Historian Victor Davis Hanson reports that:

> No exact record exists of the number of Tlaxcalans killed or captured – no doubt the dead were more than a thousand. Further Allied Indian reinforcements were miles away. The tiny Spanish garrison at Vera Cruz was incommunicado. All in all, Cortez figure he had lost 70 percent of the scores and 65percent of his men. Worse still, he was more than 150 miles from the first friendly town of Tlaxcala. Had he any allies left? For the moment he was at the shore of the seemingly still neutral city of Tlacopalan (Hanson, 2003)

3.3 Escape and the Siege of Tenochtitlan

Clearly, it was going to take a major effort for the Spaniards to capture the Aztec capital. However, at this point a new development appeared that worked in Cortez's favor. There had been a devastating outbreak of smallpox the previous September through November among the Aztecs. As many as 20,000–30,000 of the Aztec population may have died during the 2 years Cortez was fighting in Mexico. By the beginning of April 1521, the Spanish—most of whom had developed some degree of immunity from the disease—managed to put together a new force with which to lay siege to Tenochtitlan. The new Army consisted of just under a thousand Spanish infantry armed with crossbows and muskets, a small contingent of cavalry, and 18 cannons. Cortez also assembled an impressive army of native allies including a large contingent of Tlaxcalans.

While he was gathering men for his new Army, Cortez had his men construct 13 "Brigantine ships" that could carry troops across Lake Texcoco. These boats were more than 40 feet long and 9 feet at the beam. They could be powered by either sails or paddles and they drew only 2 feet of water; a feature which made them extremely mobile in the shallow waters of the lake. Each boat could carry 25 men, together with several horses. The Brigantines made it easy for Cortez to move his men around the lake and attack the city in many places without having to rely on bridges.[3]

The siege of Tenochtitlan lasted just over 3 months. When the last Aztec resistance had finally been subdued, the Spanish invaders began a systematic destruction of all the various ceremonial forums and buildings in the Aztec capital. They replaced them with new buildings that formed a city which became the capital for "New Spain" and Hernan Cortez became the governor of New Spain before he retired had returned to his home in Spain."

It is difficult to overstate the significance of Cortez's accomplishments in conquering the Aztec empire. In the decades after he defeated the Aztecs, a variety of Spanish explorers inspired by Cortez pushed Spain to expand its claim of territory in North America all the way to the border of the English colony of Canada in the north and to the Mississippi River to the east by the end of the sixteenth century.

3.4 Francisco Pizzaro and Diego Almagro

The next adventurer to expand the Spanish Empire in America was Francisco Pizzaro. Born in 1478 to a poor family in Castile, Spain, Pizzaro had spent the early years of his adult life working with expeditions to explore the Spanish discoveries in the New World. He was with the expedition in 1519 led by Vasco de Balboa which discovered the Pacific Ocean no the West Coast of the Isthmus of Panama. Soon after that expedition, Spanish explorer Pedro Arias de Avila founded Panama City on the Pacific shore of the Isthmus of Panama. The city quickly became a major financial center for the growing Spanish trade with the Orient. Pizzaro had managed to achieve a position of considerable wealth for his service with the Spanish forces, and became mayor of the city for 2 years. In March 1526 he formed a partnership with Diego Almagro to fund a group to explore the Pacific coast of South America. A third partner, Hernando de Luque, served as a silent banker for the group.

3.5 Pizzaro and Almagro Invade Peru

In November 1526 Pizzaro and Almagro left Panama City with about 600 men and two ships. After arriving at the Pacific coast of South America the two men split up. Almagro headed back to Panama City to get reinforcements, while another group, headed by Bartolome Ruiz, who was the group's head pilot, sailed south to explore the coast of Peru. The rest of the men stayed with Pizzaro on a small island near the mouth of the San Juan River. When Ruiz returned from his exploration of the southern coast, he reported that he had captured a large balsa raft that was apparently on a mission to barter Inca artifacts with natives along the coast. The raft was carrying a variety of valuable items, including elaborate gold and silver trinkets that were clearly the product of sophisticated civilization that was located further inland. Pizzaro wasted no time in sending a report to King Charles that described in great detail what Ruiz had discovered, and arguing that this area would be worth exploring.

Before they could do that, they needed additional support for a larger exploration of Peru, and the supporters of the project back in Panama City had decided that Pizzaro's adventures were not meeting with success and that the entire project should be abandoned. They sent word to Pizzaro that he and his men should come home. However, Pizzaro had no intention of abandoning his position. When the ship from Panama City came to take the stranded men home, he refused to go. Gathering his men together he drew his sword and traced a line in the sand with one side of the line representing a decision to return to Panama City and the other side a decision to stay where they were. Pointing to the Peru side of the line, he said, "Here lies Peru with its riches" Pointing to the other side he added "here is Panama and its poverty." "Choose, each man, what best becomes a brave Castilian. For my part I stay here [in Peru]." Only 13 men crossed the line to stay in Peru and wait for reinforcements and suppliers from Panama City.

Since supporters in Panama City were reluctant to offer any support for the invasion of South America, it was decided that Pizzaro should return to Spain to get support from King Charles I. When Pizzaro got to Spain, he was able to get an audience with the young king. Charles was impressed with Pizzaro's argument that Peru would be a worthwhile addition to the Spanish Empire in America. The king gave Pizzaro a license to "discover and conquer Peru." If Pizzaro succeeded, he would be appointed governorate of a newly created province of New Castile, which stretched for 600 miles south of Panama City along the west coast of Peru. At the same time, the King indicated that Diego Almagro would be appointed governorate of New Toledo, which would be a new province south of New Castile.

Following his session with the king, Pizzaro returned to Panama City to join his partners and redouble their efforts to recruit Spanish troops so that they could return to Peru and invade the Incan Empire. Hernan Cortez had managed to destroy the Aztec Empire by capturing their capital city of Tenochtitlan and deposing the Emperor Montezuma. Francisco Pizzaro and Diego Almagro faced a more formidable task in their efforts to destroy the Incan Empire. When the Spaniards arrived in Peru in February of 1532 the Incans were in the last stage of a civil war between two brothers to see who their new leader would be. With an army that numbered about 200 infantrymen and some cavalry, Pizzaro took his time moving southwards along the western coast of South America. By mid-November he had reached the town of Cajamarca, where he invited the new Incan leader, Atahuala, to come to a meeting.

Atahuala came to the meeting without realizing that he had walked into a trap. Pizzaro had taken advantage of the situation to set an ambush that allowed him to capture Atahuala and force his army to move west into the mountains. Pizarro then demanded that Atahuala must provide a sizable ransom for his freedom. The Incan leader agreed to fill a room that measured 22 feet long by 17 feet wide and reached the height of 8 feet, with articles of gold. However, even though Atahuala met this demand, Pizzaro's colleagues still did not trust the Incan leader, accusing him of murdering his brother, Huscar, and plotting treason against Pizzaro. Pizzaro reluctantly agreed to have Atahuala executed, and he appointed one of his generals to replace him as ruler of the Incan Empire. With a puppet Emperor in place, Pizzaro was ready to attack the Incan capital city of Cusco. He gathered a force that included 100 cavalry and a handful of infantrymen. He moved south along the Peruvian coast and finally entered Cusco on November 15, 1533.

3.6 Pizzaro and Almagro Fight for Cusco

Pizzaro was now in control of the Incan capital. However, the Incans had learned how to deal with the Spanish cavalry in the mountainous areas of southern Peru, and they were prepared to fight to regain control of their capital. Cusco was located in the southwestern corner of New Castile, only a few miles north of the border between New Castile and the neighboring province of New Toledo. Both Francisco Pizzaro and Diego Almagro laid claim to the city as part of their territorial authority and both considered themselves to be the representative of the Spanish Crown's authority in Peru.

In May of 1536, an Incan Army laid siege to the city of Cuzco. The defenders of the city, who supported Pizzaro, were able to hold off the attacking Inca forces until troops under Almagro's command arrived with reinforcements that forced the Incas to lift the siege. There were now two Spanish forces vying for control of Cuzco. Pizzaro had superior forces, and on April 26, 1538 their troops were able to defeat the Almagro forces at the battle of La Salina just outside of Cuzco and take Diego Almagro prisoner. Needless to say, he was promptly executed and Francisco Pizzaro's forces were left in control of Peru. However, as was frequently the case with imperial adventures, Pizzaro's victory was short-lived. In June of 1541 a group of Almagro's followers—including Almagro's son—attacked Pizzaro in his home and murdered him while he was eating breakfast.

The Incans continued to resist the efforts of Spain to control the remainder of their Empire by retreating westward into the mountains where they could better resist the Spanish troops. The Viceroy of Peru was not finally established until 1572 when the last gasp of the Inca opposition had been defeated. By the end of the sixteenth century the Spanish Empire stretched from the borders of the English colonies of North America to the tip of South America (see Fig. 3.1).

In the middle of this vast empire was the Isthmus of Panama, a narrow strip of land which offered merchants the cheapest route for moving their goods between Europe and the Orient. All this had greatly reduced the cost of shipping goods between Spain and the Orient. Except for one basic problem. Merchants needed money to finance their trade, and at the end of the sixteenth century the only medium of exchange serving as an international "money" that was widely available throughout the world were coins that were cast from gold or silver. Unfortunately, both of these metals were in very short supply throughout Europe. As historian Mark Cartwright put it, "if all the gold in Europe at that time had been collected together in one place, it would've taken up the volume of a mere 2 m (6-foot) sided cube."[4] Even if Cartwright's estimate of the amount of gold available in the fifteenth century is grossly wide of the mark, it suggests that what was desperately needed to support the large volume of global trade, was an enormous increase in the supply of precious metals.

Incredibly, that is exactly what happened!

3.7 The Discovery of Gold in New Spain

We have seen that the search for precious metals—especially gold—was the most important objective of European *Conquistadors* coming to the New World. Christopher Columbus had quickly concluded that the natives who greeted him upon his arrival at San Salvador Island must have had some access to gold because of the jewelry they wore. However, no one was able (or perhaps no one was willing) to tell him where the gold needed to make those trinkets had come from. Explorations of areas near villages that might have gold did not reveal any precious metals, so the Spaniards continued to look elsewhere.

Persistence can have its rewards. In 1545 the search for precious metals was rewarded with the discovery of significant gold deposits around the Mexican town of Zacatecas. At about the same time, a huge deposit of silver was discovered in a mountain of silver just outside Potosí, Bolivia. Over the next two decades additional sites of gold or silver were discovered that added to the output of precious metals in the Spanish Empire. The gold and silver that came from all of these mines was turned into ingots and coins that were sent to Havana and the Spanish peso became the money used in the international marketplace, and within the space of a few years Spain became the source of precious metals throughout the Western World. However,

3.7 The Discovery of Gold in New Spain

Fig. 3.1 The Spanish Empire circa 1700. *Sources* Thomas (2005), Walton (1994), Cartwright (2021) and Martin and Parker (2022)

although the huge supply of precious metals vastly increased the supply of money in the international marketplace, it brought a new problem for the merchant fleets carrying precious metals to their final destination. The gold and silver coins and ingots traveled to a variety of commercial markets, and in the uncertain world of pirates and international rivalries, how could the Spanish merchants protect their gold shipments?

3.8 The Spanish Treasure Fleets

To meet this challenge the Spanish organized what became known as "Treasure Fleets" to manage their shipments of goods and money. Rather than having individual merchant ships sail by themselves. the merchants could travel to Havanna, Seville, or Manilla, where they could join 20 or 30 other Spanish ships to form a convoy of merchant ships that would form a fleet of ships which could be accompanied in their trip across the Atlantic Ocean by Spanish warships that could ward off would-be be attackers. These "Treasure Fleets" as they were known as, were very effective. The key to their success was the large Spanish warships that carried 20 to 30 cannons and a crew of 200 seamen and 100 soldiers to board an enemy.

Figure 3.2 shows how the treasure fleets operated. The gold or silver coins and ingots were sent directly to Havana. From there they would be loaded onto ships in a fleet headed for either Manilla or Seville. When they reached their destination, the ships would unload their precious cargos and be ready to return to Havana with goods from the Orient or from Europe on the next treasure fleet. In a normal year there would be two treasure fleets completing round trips to Spain and the Philippines. The Treasure Fleets were a huge success. Historian Timothy Walton estimates that during the period they were in operation, gold and silver from the mines of the Spanish Empire supplied more than 4 billion pesos of precious metals. This was about 80 percent of the world's silver production and 70% of the world's gold output.[5]

The discovery of gold and silver in New Spain made the Spanish Empire in the Americas the most successful example of imperialism in the early modern era. As a result of their destruction of the Aztec and Inca Empires and the discovery of a huge source of precious metals at Zacatecas and Potosí, Spain grew from a modest player in the economic and political world of Europe into the most powerful empire of the sixteenth and seventeenth centuries. But all of this did little to change the agrarian economy of Spain itself. By the end of the nineteenth century the gold and silver mines were largely exhausted, and the Spanish government could no longer maintain the cost of being a major power in European politics. The wars in Europe drained the Spanish Crown's treasury and brought little if any benefit to the average Spaniard and the Spanish were having to deal with two new countries that were entering the imperial world of North America.

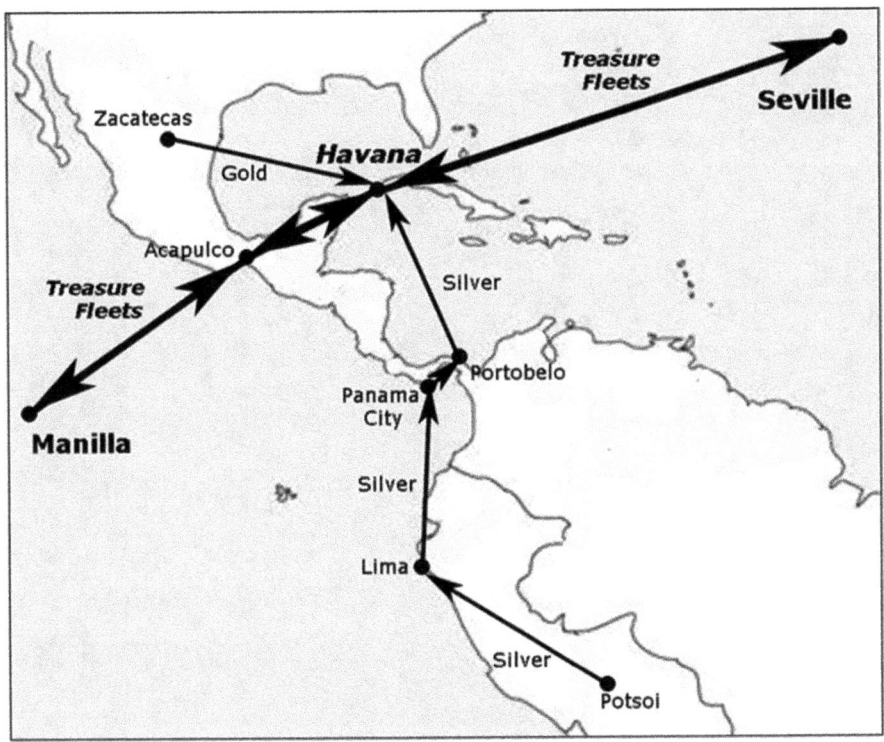

Fig. 3.2 The Spanish treasure ships. *Sources* Cartwright (2021)

Notes

1. The estimates of the size of Cortez's force very slightly; the figures cited in the text are from Thomas (2005).
2. This is the number commonly given for the population of Tenchtitlan. All of the estimates of the size of towns and Aztec forces are based on contemporary reports which tended to grossly exaggerate the size of the indigenous forces. Thomas (2005) argues that the Aztecs capital was probably bigger than any city in Spain and that the Spanish forces were generally outnumbered in their new military encounters.
3. The description of the brigantine boats and the success of Cortez in assembling a new Army draws upon the work of Hanson (2001).
4. Cartwright (2024).
5. Walton (1994, 189) Walton's book is the most extensive treatment of Spanish gold and silver production during the era of the Treasure Fleets.

Chapter 4
The Spanish Armada

The treasure fleets were successful in protecting the movement of goods and money from Havana to either Manilla or Seville. But there was still considerable commercial activity that was not included in the treasure fleets, and these ships were subject to constant threats from a variety of pirates; many of whom were quietly supported by the governments of England; France, Portugal; or the Dutch. One of the most famous English pirates was Sir Francis Drake. Drake was an Englishman who had acquired a reputation as someone who had been active and very successful in the slave trade and as a pirate raiding Spanish ships.

4.1 Queen Elizabeth's Secret Plan

Drake had also managed to become a favorite of Queen Elizabeth, who early in the fall of 1577 met with him to discuss an expedition that was to be kept a secret from everyone else. The Queen wanted Drake to sail around the world terrorizing Spanish ships and ports and hopefully returning to England with some treasure. Since Spain and England were maintaining an uneasy relationship with pirates like Drake, who were not formally recognized by the English Crown, Elizabeth could not formally sanction the actual purpose of the voyage that she wanted Drake to undertake. In fact, she insisted that only the two of them would know the true destinations of the voyage. The details of what the Queen wanted Drake to do are imperfectly preserved in a document in the British Library. Roughly stated, the instructions said that Drake should sail through the Strait of Magellan and then proceed north along the West Coast of South America to collect to raid the Spanish traffic and collect "gold, silver, spices, ... and divers other commodities." The entire trip was expected to take 13 months.[1]

The announced purpose of Drake's voyage was very different, this was billed as a voyage to harass Spanish shipping around the Straits of Panama. He agreed to keep the true purpose of the trip a secret, partly because he was worried that if his crew knew that the real purpose of their voyage would involve sailing through the Strait of Magellan, he would have trouble recruiting seamen. He spent the better part of a year putting together his expedition. When completed, the fleet included 5 ships. *Pelican*, which was the flagship designed by Drake. It was built to be a small Galleon, weighing 139 tons, carrying a crew of 80 and 13 cannons of varying caliber. *Pelican* was renamed *Goldin Hind* in 1578, and was the only ship to return to England in 1580. A second war ship, *Elizabeth*, was the only other ship in the group carrying any cannons. Slightly smaller than *Pelican*, *Elizabeth* did not survive the trip through the Strait of Magellan. Three other ships went along as supply vessels, but did not stay with Drake for the entire trip.

4.2 Drake's Voyage Around the World

In June of 1577 Drake set forth with the Queen's blessing to sail around the world and see what he could find. The fleet immediately encountered storms that forced them to turn back to Plymouth for repairs that took most of the rest of the year to repair. They finally left Plymouth on December 15th 1577 to head south west across the Atlantic to the Cape Verde Islands. From there they headed across the Atlantic and sailed south along the east coast of Brazil. By Christmas day they had reached Cape Horn at the tip of South America, and were prepared to go through the Strait of Magellan.

The trip through the Strait took a heavy toll on Drake's party. By the time they reached the Pacific Ocean, only *the Golden Hind* was still seaworthy. Nevertheless, Drake was determined to carry on. As he sailed along the Western coast of South America, he discovered that the Spanish towns had little or no defense against a well-armed warship. The *Golden Hind* had no problems replenishing supplies when needed, and Drake's men were able to get small amounts of silver and gold. In February of 1579 they paid a visit to Lima, the capital of Peru and while visiting with Spanish officers, Drake heard that a Spanish Treasure Ship—*Cacafuego*—had left port a few days earlier loaded with gold and silver.

After a short chase, the *Golden Hind* had no trouble catching up with their slow-moving prey, and as they pulled alongside *Cacafuego* the English fired a single broadside. The surprised Spanish captain quickly ordered his men to surrender and allow the English to board their ship. Drake managed to find a quiet bay where the two ships could anchor and the English sailors could eagerly transfer the treasure from *Cacafuego to the Golden Hind. It took Drake and his men six days to move the gold and silver treasure on board the Cacafuego to the Golden Hind. "This fact alone,"* historian Steven Cootes notes, *"suggests the quantity of treasures seized was prodigious."* Spanish officers agreed that *" there were gold silver bars and silver coins aboard to the value of 362,000 pesos" together with 40,000 pieces of gold and silver and 14 chests crammed with gold and silver coins"*.[2]

At this point Drake decided it was time to go home. He had collected enough gold and silver and done enough damage to Spanish Prestige to satisfy the Queen's appetite. In the hope that he might find a way to avoid sailing through the Indian Ocean and around South Africa, Drake continued to sail north past the ismuth of Panama and Baja California and the California coast. There is some confusion about exactly how far North he actually went. We know that he reached the San Francisco Bay region, and we know that he stopped long enough to claim it for England. There is general agreement that he reached the sand dunes further north on the Oregon coast. Historian Samuel Bawlf claims that a gap in Drake's journals suggests he got as far north as Alaska in his search for a Northwest Passage back to Europe.[3]

Eventually, as it began to get colder and colder every day, and he did not find signs of a Northwest Passage, Drake headed across the Pacific towards the Spice Islands. He reached the Philippines and stopped long enough to pick up some valuable spices to take back to Elizabeth. From there he followed roughly the same route as the Magellan El Cano passage took in 1518. The Goldin Hind arrived home to London and was met by a jubilant crowd on September 26th 1580.

Francis Drake's voyage around the world remains one of the more remarkable accomplishments in maritime history. Over the course of 3 years, he managed to become the second explorer to circle the globe in a single trip. He collected enough treasure to more than cover the cost of repaying Queen Elizabeth's public debt and there was still enough left to pay investors of the trip. He had terrified Spanish officials into realizing that a single warship could easily attack and capture ships anywhere along the western coast of their South American empire. And he infuriated Phillip II, the king of Spain, who immediately turned his full attention to the creation of a military force that could bring England to her knees, and restore the prestige of the Spanish Empire.

Yet, for all this success, Francis Drake remains something of an enigma to historians. On the one hand he receives plaudits for successfully circumnavigating the globe and bringing home enough stolen treasure to finance the English government for a year. Queen Elizabeth was sufficiently impressed with his accomplishments that she knighted him. However, Drake's early success in the slave trade and his career as a pirate has caused him to lose favor with some twentieth-century historians, who portray him as someone more interested in promoting his own reputation rather than serving England's needs. Be that as it may, Drake proved to be an excellent public relations figure for Elizabeth and his treasure financed her government at a time when she sorely needed some financial help.

4.3 The Spanish Armada and the Invasion of England

One person who was not favorably impressed with Francis Drake's accomplishments in 1578 was King Philip II of Spain. Philip was the ruler of a vast Empire that stretched from Eastern Europe to the tip of South America. Spanish troops were waging a vigorous battle to subdue Dutch uprising in the Netherlands, and the last thing Phillip needed at this point was to have a rampaging English pirate demonstrate that the western half of the Spanish Empire in America was virtually undefended.

Even before Drake had completed his trip, Philip was working on a plan to deal with the English menace. The basic element of the Spanish plan seemed simple enough. A fleet of 130 Spanish ships—including more than 90 warships—would gather at Lisbon Harbor. This "Armada" of ships would enter the West end of the English Channel and move east along the Channel towards Calais, France. When they reached Calais, the Armada would join a force of Spanish soldiers in the Netherlands waiting to invade England.

The Spanish Plan was simple enough on when put on paper, however the movement of such a large fleet of ships proved to be a far more difficult challenge. The Spanish warships were slow-moving galleons which were designed to engage enemy ships at close quarters. It took more than two days just to get the boats out of Lison Harbor. Once they were in the Channel, they maintained a formation that was a broad crescent that could protect the fleet from English attacks, but the ships had to move very slowly to maintain their formations. The English ships were smaller and faster than the Spanish, and they used their artillery to damage enemy ships with hit and run attacks from a distance rather than getting close to board their enemy. The main English objective was to protect the coastline of southern England and inflict as much damage as they could on the Spanish fleet before it could join the troops waiting for an invasion.

Figure 4.1 depicts a series of encounters between the two fleets that began on July 31st, 1558, with the appearance of the Spanish fleet at the western end of the English Channel. The Spanish managed to fight their way slowly towards Calais, where they hoped to connect with a Spanish invasion force waiting to cross the channel and invade England. The English ships persisted in attacking the rear of the Spanish formation to damage enemy ships and protect their southern coast. Neither side had much luck sinking enemy ships, and the Spanish fleet finally succeeded in reaching Calais on August 6th.

However, at this point the Spanish plan began to fall apart. Both sides were running out of ammunition and water, and the Duke of Parma was unwilling to bring his troops to Calais, where they could be ferried across the channel. The English attacks on Spanish ships blocked efforts by the Armada to return to Lisbon via the English Channel. The Spanish ships were therefore forced to dock at Calais. On the evening of August 8th, the English launched an attack of fire ships which forced the Spanish ships to scatter north along the Dutch coast (See Fig. 4.1). With their formations widely dispersed the only option left for individual Spanish ships that wanted to return to Spain was to have each ship find its own way back to Lisbon. Most chose to sail north of Scotland and turn south along the west coast of Ireland towards Lisbon. While this offered a way to get back to Lisbon, it proved to be a very dangerous alternative because of the weather. Storms along the Irish coast caused at least 24 ships to be lost due to the bad weather, and forced others to look further up the coast for a place to find a friendly port.[4]

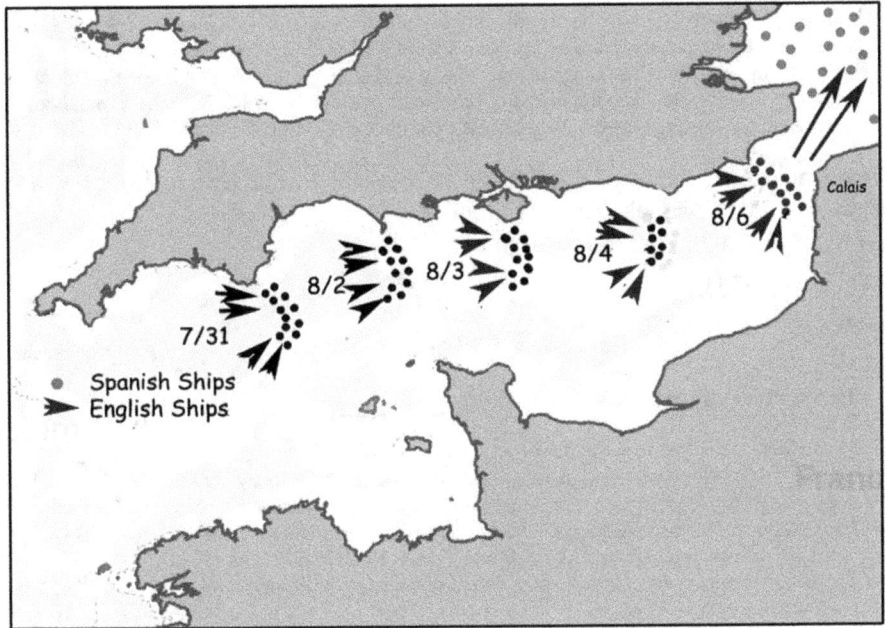

Fig. 4.1 The battles in the English channel. *Sources* Martin and Parker (2022)

4.4 The Defeat of the Armada

The "defeat" of the Spanish Armada was a serious blow to the prestige of the Spanish Empire, but it was hardly the end of Spanish naval domination in the seventeenth-century world economy. Many of the Armada ships eventually found their way home or to a friendly port; and Spanish treasure fleets continued to ship gold between Spain, Panama, and the Orient for as long as the mines in the Spanish Empire could continue to produce gold and silver. Phillip II was able to use the precious metals in New Spain finance to his religious wars against the protestants in the Netherlands. The most significant change to emerge from the Armada's demise was that the English were able to flex their muscles to deflect the Spanish invasion threat to their Island. It would be some time before the English became major players in the East Indies trade, however Queen Elizabeth got things going in 1603 by investing part of her share of the booty from Drake's trip around the world in the creation of a joint stock company that would eventually emerge as the East India Company. Historian Laurance Bergreen notes that the economist John Maynard Keynes, writing in 1930, expressed the conviction that:

> Drake's lust for gold and silver heralded the birth of the British Empire and the modern British economy. "I trace the beginnings of British foreign investment to the treasure which Drake stole from Spain in 1580. In that year he returned to England bringing with him the prodigious spoils of the Golden Hind. Queen Elizabeth was a considerable shareholder in the syndicate which had financed the expedition." Keynes enumerated the benefits Drake's

treasure purchased. "Out of her share she paid off the whole of England's foreign debt, balanced her Budget, and found herself with about £40,000 in hand. Thus she invested in the Levant Company—which prospered. Out of the profits of the Levant Company, the East India Company was founded; and the profits of this great enterprise were the were the foundation of England's subsequent foreign investment. [5](Bergreen, 1978. 394)

Simply put Keynes believed that Drake's voyage laid the foundation for the creation of what would become the British Empire.

Notes

1. The details of the Queen's instructions are taken from Coote (2003).
2. Coote (2003).
3. The search for a "Northwest Passage" which would allow the English and other northern European states to reach the Orient by a sea route across what today we know as Canada, had been going on for some time. For a discussion of Drake's interest in finding such a route, see Bawlf (2003). The discussion of Drakes' other accomplishments over the course of his voyage in the text draws upon Bergreen (2024) and Coote (2003) and Walton (1994).
4. There is an extensive literature dealing with the adventures of Francis Drake, the battles between the English and Spanish control of the English Channel and the problems of the Spanish Armada following the battles in the channel. The definitive work is Martin and Parker (2022); also see Mattingly (1963), Andrews (1984), and Coote (2003).
5. Bergreen (1978, 394).

Chapter 5
The East India Company and the British Empire

5.1 Inventing the Joint Stock Company

The joint stock company created by the Queen of England in 1601 was a new form of financial organization that combined shares from private investors along with funds invested by the state in a single joint stock company. Since the state was one of the partners, the newly created East India Company [EIC] was given the authority of the state—including the power to wage war, if that was a necessary action to protect the EIC's trade interests. The English were not the only country to form a joint stock company that included both private and public investors. In 1602, one year later, the Dutch created an East India Company that was very successful in attracting the East Indies trading markets. In addition to being huge private financial institutions, these EIC's maintained private armies that were as large as the national armies of England or the Dutch Republics.

In 1707, nearly a hundred years after the start of British East India Company [BEIC] activities in India, the Mughal Emperor of the Indian peninsula at the time, Aurangzeb, died. His last words, "after me, chaos" would soon prove true. What happened next was a brutal power struggle as all of Aurangzeb's many potential heirs competed for control over the Empire. Even after this power struggle the new "Emperor" was imprisoned, and his heir was cast out from the Mughal's traditional seat of power in Delhi. During this period the only real government authority came from the rulers of cities who both realized that the ensuing chaos meant taxes and tributes no longer needed to be paid.

One of these rulers was the BEIC, who had made a foothold for themselves in the city of Calcutta, which had become a sort of charter city. From here they were able to slowly expand their power and operations as fortuitous happenings and anarchy left them mostly untouched and able to steadily continue their production.

With the collapse of ordered Mughal forces the BEIC was left as one of the more significant military forces in the region. As such, when Persians and Afghans began to invade the weakened Mughal State many civilians were left refugees who fled into the arms of waiting BEIC governed cities. The introduction of new workers and the capital they carried was one of the first of many advantages the company would gain in the long anarchy period.

The Ruler of Bengal at the time further aided the BEIC simply by being unlikeable. When the Company and this ruler, Siraj ud-daula, came into rivalry and conflict many of the people around Siraj immediately betrayed him. His General's having outright abandoned him on the eve of battle left the gates wide open for the British East India company to swoop in and establish itself in a position of power.

Time and again the BEIC would make significant fortuitous gains like this simply because anyone who could or would be a rival to them was dragged down by internal issues or external pressures that the BEIC did not have to consider. This, combined with the fact that the BEIC consistently had a much higher pay scale compared to its competitors, meant that the company was seen as trustworthy at the time. So much so that by 1765 the Company had been given the right to raise their own taxes on the former citizens of the Mughal Empire. Taking what should be the power of the emperor onto themselves and in doing so making the Company an imperial asset of Great Britain. This notable power was, of course, eventually noticed by the British government. Despite much pushing back and forth, the company was drawn closer and closer to the government, accepting a bailout in 1772 during a Famine and eventually having a government oversight board assigned to it in 1784.

With the oversight board in place and the company slowly having its authority taken by the British government, the company was made to focus less and less on economy and finances and pushed more into being an arm of the state complete with a standing army. What had started as a purely economic push of private imperialism had turned again to the state use of power to complete a country's Imperial ambitions.

By the end of the nineteenth century the BEIC had managed to conquer the Indian Economy. Historian Dalrymple describes the success of the East India Company:

> We still talk about the British conquering India, but that phrase disguises a more sinister reality. It was not the British government that began seizing great chunks of India in the mid-eighteenth century, but a dangerously unregulated private company headquartered in one small office, five windows wide, in London, and managed in India by a violent, utterly ruthless and intermittently mentally unstable corporate predator – Clive. India's transition to colonialism took place under a for-profit corporation, which existed entirely for the purpose of enriching its investors.[1]

Table 5.1 gives us a feel for the success of the East India Companies of Britain, and the Dutch in importing textiles from India.

All of this raises the issue of who paid for the British imperialism in India. Cliometricians Lance Davis and Robert Huttenback have provided the most complete attempt to measure gains and losses from British Imperialism in their book *Mammon and the Pursuit of Empire*. They argue that while it is clear that Britain as a whole did not benefit economically from their Empire, many individual investors managed to gather substantial returns.[2] For others, Davis and Huttenback find that the costs and benefits varied, but their data make it clear that the British public paid considerably more than they received from the far-fetched regions of the Empire. Like the Spanish

Table 5.1 Textile exports from India; 1665–1760

Years	EIC (total exports)	VOC (total exports)	Exports total
1665–1669	139,977	126,572	266,249
1670–1674	510,521	257,918	768,439
1675–1679	569,547	127,459	697,006
1680–1684	967,784	283,456	1251,140
1685–1689	614,426	316,167	930,593
1690–1694	171,887	156,891	328,778
1695–1699	387,523	364,613	752,136
1700–1704	597,978	310,611	908,589
1705–1709	204,014	294,886	498,900
1710–1714	575,102	372,601	947,703
1715–1719	534,188	435,923	970,111
1720–1724	796,293	475,752	1272,045
1725–1729	821,312	399,477	1220,789
1730–1734	727,816	241,070	968,886
1735–1739	784,672	315,543	1,100,215
1740–1744	812,700	288,050	1100,750
1745–1749	684,188	262,261	946,449
1750–1754	632,174	532,865	1,169,039
1755–1759	470,192	321,251	791,443

Indian exports of textiles to Europe (pieces per year)

before them, the British found that Imperialism was an expensive proposition. Like the Spanish, they pressed on with efforts to expand their imperial empire regardless.

Notes

1. Dalrymple (1919) offers the best source for the success of the EIC in taking over India.
2. See Davis and Huttenback (1986, p. 30).

Chapter 6
The American Revolution

6.1 British and French Rivalry in Canada

One of the most unusual examples of an imperialist war in the early modern era was the conflict between Great Britain and its Thirteen American Colonies at the end of the eighteenth century. A war that began in 1776 eventually involved France and Spain as allies of the Americans. And this is one of the few examples where imperialistic rivalries produced a war where the victims of an imperial policy—the Colonial Americans—were able to free themselves from the grip of imperial policy imposed by the interferences of a colonial powers—in this case the British Empire.

Since the beginning of the eighteenth century the British government had pursued a policy of encouraging settlement in the East Coast of the North American Continent that was hugely successful. By 1776 the population of the American Colonies had grown to about 2.5 million people, and a bustling system of trade had emerged involving Great Britain, Colonial America, and the rest of the world. At the heart of the quarrel between colonists and the British were a series of "Navigation Acts" intended to control and monitor the trade activity of her colonies. These acts were part of a larger system of mercantilism pursued by the British government, and they created a good deal of irritation on the part of the colonists, who objected to the efforts Parliament to control their economy.[1] Together with the efforts of the British to impose taxes on the colonies, the difficulties between colonists and King George III's government led to a war that began with the battle of Bunker Hill just outside of Boston in June of 1776. The war that followed lasted for just over eight years and eventually ended with a victory for the colonists at Yorktown, Virginia when Lord Cornwallis surrendered the last British Army in the colonies to George Washington's army of French and American troops.

6.2 The 10 Battles of Saratoga, New York

Though the war lasted for 8 years, most historians agree that the eventual colonial victory was decided by a series of engagements that were fought in the summer and fall of 1777 in upstate New York.[2] The war started with the Declaration of Independence issued by the Continental Congress on July 4, 1776. On August 23rd the British Parliament declared the colonists to be in "open and avowed rebellion," and it ordered officials to use their utmost efforts to suppress such a rebellion.

The British plan for an early victory in the war; concocted by general John Burgoyne, was a complex plan for a three-pronged attack to push the colonial forces in upstate New York south along the Lake Champlain and the Hudson River all the way to New York City. They would then link up with another British force under General Howe to attack the colonial army in New York City under the command of George Washington. Unfortunately for Burgoyne, Howe did not accept the plan, preferring to attack Philadelphia instead of New York.

Despite the confusion associated with disagreements on the part of their generals, Burgoyne proceeded with the plan. On July 2nd an army of British troops 6700 regulars, half of them Hessians, about 700 Canadians, and 500 native warriors encountered their first contact with colonial troops at Fort Ticonderoga. This proved to be the first of ten struggles between the two sides as British troops stubbornly fought their war south down along the Hudson River. The colonials abandoned Fort Ticonderoga; however, they managed to slow the British advance, and a series of short battles in July and August brought the two armies to the town of Bennington, Vermont, by August 16th.[3]

The encounter at Bennington was an important prelude to the larger battle of Saratoga that began on September 19th. The British, who were running out of both men and supplies, were hoping to capture supplies stored at the Bennington depot. Instead, they ran into an American force of colonial militia that forced them to withdraw after suffering major casualties and 900 men surrendered. The British did not get their supplies, and the battle had further slowed their advance down to Albany on their way to New York city.

It all came down to whether the British forces could defeat the colonial forces just south of the city of Saratoga. The Americans had built formidable defenses on Bemis Heights, which overlooked the Hudson River. On September 19th the British attacked the entrenched American troops and were sharply rebuffed with heavy losses. General John Burgoyne's only hope now was for British reinforcements, but none were forthcoming. On October 17th Burgoyne' army surrendered his forces to the American General Horatio Gates.

6.3 Implications of the Battles of Saratoga

The American victory at Saratoga came at a particularly favorable time for the Colonists. The loss of an entire British army to American forces had a dramatic effect on the way European powers particularly France, viewed Britain's colonial exploits—as France and Britain were still recovering from a seven-year war from 1754–63 that Americans know as the French and Indian Wars. Britain and her colonial allies won those conflicts, and the Treaty of Paris signed in 1763 forced France to give up virtually all of her Canadian Territories to the British. Michael Clodfleter notes that:

> But more important than the numbers of Saratoga was the image – one of an Army of the world's foremost colonial power surrendering en mass to colonial rebels – an image very tempting very pleasing to a France still smarting stained of defeat in the loss of an Empire to other. British Armies. (Clodfelter, 2015, 138)

Louis XVI, the French king, decided that his country would join the Americans in the fight against the British. On February 6, 1778, Benjamin Franklin and his two colleagues in Paris managed to negotiate an agreement between France and the Americans pledging France to send supplies and military aid to the colonists during the fight with the British.

It is difficult to overstate the importance of the alliance with France during the war. Simply put, the Americans could not win this war without help from their European allies. They did not have the industrial base to produce arms and supplies for their troops or the financial resources to pay for them. European countries—and particularly France—were willing to sell supplies and accept debt from the Continental Congress to pay for them. Though the Americans had a small Navy, there was no way that they could seriously interfere with the British Navy's ability to move troops and supplies support their war effort. The French proved as good as their word. In addition to sending supplies for the Continental Army, two regiments of French soldiers fought with the rebels throughout the rest of the war, and the French Navy actively interfered with the operations of the British fleet. In fact, it was a fleet of French warships that kept the British fleet from reinforcing the troops under General Cornwallis and his troops at York Town in 1781. Cornwallis surrendered to Washington's army on October 19, 1781. His surrender marked the end of the fighting in the war, but it took another two years of negotiating to work out the details that would end the war. An armistice was formally announced on January 20, 1783, after Britain, France, and the United States finally agreed on terms. On September 3, 1783, Britain, France, and the American Congress finally signed the Treaty of Paris, which ended the American Revolutionary War.

6.4 The War of 1812

The British reluctantly conceded that the Americans had won their independence, but they continued to find ways to harass the new nation. They forcibly took American sailors off American ships claiming they were British sailors who were deserters from the royal Navy. The British were at war with France at this point, and their efforts to block American trade with the French caused interference with American ships. Finally, Americans accused the British of supporting Indian resistance to American settlement in the Northwest Territory of the Great Lakes. None of these grievances would seem to be sufficient cause for a war, however, both countries were sufficiently irritated with each other so that they were willing to consider fighting a war to resolve their problems. On June 1, 1812, President James Madison declared war on Great Britain.

What became known to Americans as "the Second War of Independence" could at best be described as "inconclusive." The U.S. Navy performed well against the British Navy in single ship battles, but the British had far more ships and the Royal Navy was able to impose an effective blockade of the east coast for most of the war and efforts by the American Army to invade Canada did not go well. The war is best remembered by Americans for two events. First is the British invasion of Maryland after the battle of Bladensburg, in August, 1814, which allowed British troops to enter Washington D.C., and set fire to the White House, the Capitol, and other government buildings. The other is the resounding victory at the Battle of New Orleans by American troops commanded by Andrew Jackson on January 8, 1815. Jackson's victory came four months after the United States and Britain had signed the Treaty of Ghent.

The end of the war between the United States and Britain, together with defeat of Napoleon at Waterloo marked the end of an era in the history of the Western world. In a curious way, the fact that the war of 1812–14 was inconclusive meant that neither side could claim victory. The United States and Britain gradually came back together during the second half of the nineteenth century to the point that they would become firm allies in the new struggles that faced the world at the end of the nineteenth century.

Notes

1. For more on the Navigation Acts and the economic problems with British mercantilism, see Ransom (1968) and Taylor (2016).
2. The Saratoga battles have drawn great deal of attention from historians of the American Revolution. Wikipedia provides a detailed summary of the events; our account of the battles draws on the books by Richard Ketchum (1999), Taylor (2016) and Clodfelter (2015).
3. There were additional encounters between the two armies at Skenesborough on July 7th, Fort Ann on July 8th, Forth Stanwix and Orinsky on August 6th.

Chapter 7
The Napoleonic Wars

While the British and the Americans were establishing an American nation in New World, the French were trying to get some stability in their government after executing their monarch, Louis XVI in January of 1793. A coalition of neighboring states, including Austria, Prussia, Great Britain, the Dutch Republic, and Spain, attacked the French Republic, hoping to restore the French monarchy. In a series of battles that became known as the "war of the first coalition," the French forces managed to keep their enemies at bay, thanks in large part to the efforts of a general named Napoleon Bonaparte. Bonaparte was a young general who rose rapidly through the ranks of the French Army. In June of 1799, Bonaparte had returned to Paris after a successful campaign with French forces in Egypt, and he was something of a national hero. When a group of politicians staged a coup to reorganize the government, Napoleon was named a consul of France and 2 years later he managed to get himself elected to be consul for life. On December 2, 1804, he proudly crowned himself (and his wife Josefine) Emperor and Empress of the French Empire. During the period 1803 through 1813 Napoleon was able to control most or all of central Europe.

7.1 Napoleon Bonaparte and the French Imperial Empire: 1779–1814

It is perhaps not surprising that when he went to war Napoleon saw himself as a defender of the new French Nation. Despite this firm belief, the results of his conflicts always painted a much more Imperial picture. At the end of the War of the First Coalition in 1797 Netherlands were turned into the French satellite state known as the Batavian Republic, Prussia had acknowledged French control of the left bank of the Rhine, Northern Italy was transformed into several French sister states, and parts of the Holy Roman Empire had been annexed by the new French Republic. While this was an action more of the French Republic and not the new but capable

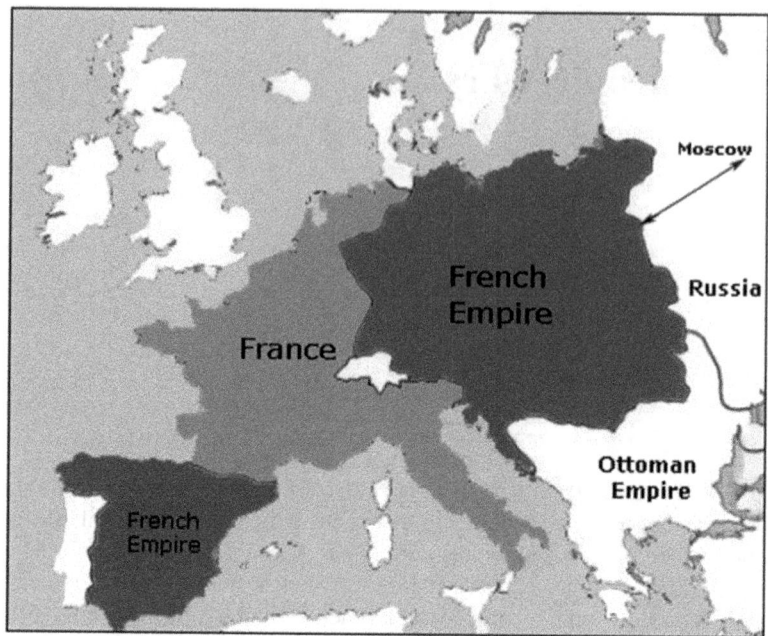

Fig. 7.1 The French empire: 1812. *Source* Clodfelter (2015)

General Napoleon, these peace treaties constantly expanded the size and power of France through Military conflict became commonplace even after Bonaparte was crowned Emperor in 1804 (Fig. 7.1).

The Wars of the 3rd, 4th, and 5th Coalition were all French victories under Emperor Napoleon Bonaparte and all of these wars added to the newly forged French Empire. Repeatedly during these wars and the earlier wars of the French Republic Napoleon had proved himself a tactical genius, often Decisively winning battles where he was predicted to lose or getting much more out of victories than would be expected. Above is a graph of some of the most significant Napoleon victories before The War of the Sixth Coalition.

By the time the war of the 5th Coalition had ended in 1809 nearly all of Europe was either part of the French Empire or paying tribute to the French in some manner thanks to the many decisive French victories under Napoleon. Austria had its Mediterranean ports seized, Prussia was surrounded and shoved into a corner of the continent. Italy was peppered throughout with French territories Northern Spain was remade part of France and Portugal was an occupied nation.

Napoleon's idea of Defending the French was quite clear. He believed that if the entirety of the continent was French there would be peace for everyone (Fig. 7.2).

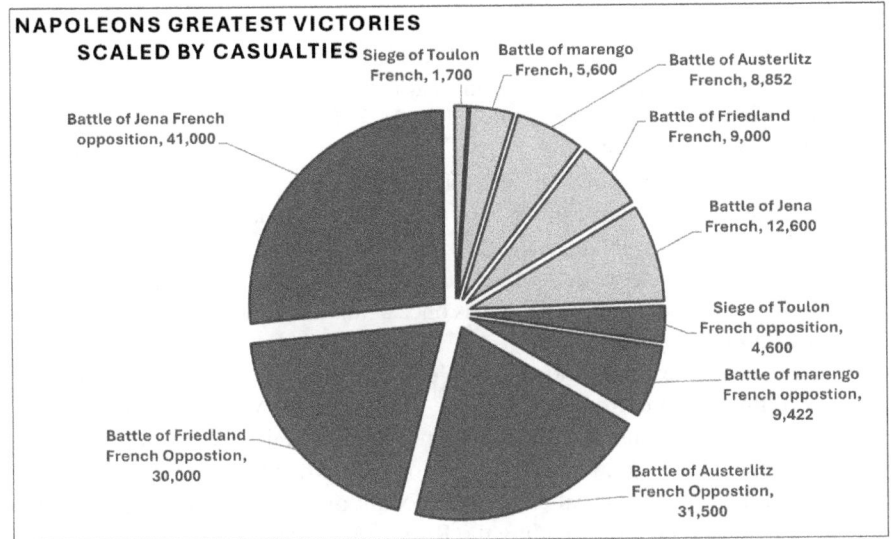

Fig. 7.2 Battles of the Napoleonic wars; 1793–1815. *Source* Clodfelter (2015)

7.2 The French Invasion of Russia

At this point the French came into conflict with Tzar Alexander I of Russia. Napoleon and Great Britain were trying to isolate each other's economy. The British were the dominant sea power, and they restricted trade with Ferance. Napoleon imposed what he called the: "Continental System" to restrict trade between Britain and the French Empire. Czar Alexander refused to restrict Russia's trade with Britain. Napoleon's reaction to this was to declare war against Russia. It proved to be a disaster for the French Empire.

In June of 1812 French troops crossed into Russia. In a series of four battles Napoleon managed to fight his way across Russia and on September 14th 1812, French forces entered Moscow. However, Czar Alexander was still not willing to go along with Napoleon's Continental System, and Napoleon found himself sitting in an abandoned city in the middle of Russia. It quickly became clear that the French army would not be able to maintain its supply lines back to Europe. With the Russian winter closing in, Napoleon reluctantly began a hasty retreat back to France on October 19th. What began as an orderly withdrawal soon became a disastrous race to return to the borders of the French Empire. In the European theater the French Army was able to find food for horses and men and the roads could handle the heavy equipment that accompanied Napoleon's troops. However, in Russia the roads were impassable, and the farms could not supply the food for French men or animals. When they left Moscow Napoleon's army had 95,000 men, 500 cannons, and 40,000 wagons. Only 10,000 men reached the Border of the French Empire.

As was his habit, Napoleon managed to quickly raise another army. But in October of 1813 the combined forces of Austria, Prussia, Sweden, and Russia dealt Napoleon's new army a decisive defeat in a battle which became known as "the battle of nations." Napoleon was forced to abdicate his position as Emperor of France, and he was exiled to the isle of Elba. In May of the next year, he managed to escape from Elba and return to France to once again raise a new army. On June 18, 1815, in what became the final battle of the Napoleonic Wars, Napoleon's troops faced the Duke of Wellington and the combined British and Prussian armies at the battle of Waterloo. The British troops held their "thin red line" against the final charge of the French Imperial Guard and Napoleon was once again forced to abdicate his position as emperor of the French Empire.

Imperial wars take many forms. Napoleon's imperial empire stands out as an example of imperialism through a series of wars which allowed France to control a number of neighboring states. On the one hand his use of military power allowed the French state to acquire additional territory. However, when he reached the border of Russia his military judgment failed to take account of either the size of the Russian state or the consequences of spending the Russian winter in Moscow.

Napoleon's imperial successes came at a considerable cost to the French people. Over the course of what historians call the "Napoleonic Wars" (1802–1815) French armies and their allies found close to a million men either killed in action or dead from disease. An additional million men suffered non-lethal casualties: many of them permanently disabled by their wounds. [1] The French population which was around thirty million people over the decade of the empire—paid a high price for their emperor's imperialism.

Note

1. The estimate of French deaths in the Napoleonic wars is from Clodfelter (2002, 192–193).

Chapter 8
The Mexican American War

At the beginning of the nineteenth century the territory of North America between the Atlantic and Pacific Oceans was divided among three political systems. The region between the Atlantic Ocean and the Mississippi River was governed by the United States of America; the region of the Pacific Northwest known as Rupert's Land or the Oregon Country was governed by the British government, and the Spanish government controlled the area called *New Spain*, which included most of the present-day states of California, Nevada, Utah, New Mexico, Arizona, and Texas. The Spanish also had jurisdiction over an area known as the *Louisiana Territory,* which stretched from the Mississippi River west to the Rocky Mountains and included the city of New Orleans (See Fig. 8.1).

8.1 The Louisiana Purchase

In 1803 Napolean Bonaparte was at the peak of his power as first consul of the newly created French Empire. His government had managed to gain control of the entire Louisiana Territory as part of an arrangement that gave Spain control of Tuscany in northern Italy and left the Louisiana Territory in the hands of Spain. Napoleon was looking for ways to finance his war with Great Britain and he was anxious to make sure that the British would not get control of the Louisiana Territory from Spain. Another leader who was anxious to control the Louisiana Territory was Thomas Jefferson, the President of the United States. Jefferson wanted to make sure that the United States would have control of the city of New Orleans at the mouth of the Mississippi River. The President had authorized Robert Livingston and James Monroe as representatives to approach the French with an offer of $9 million to buy the city. When Napoleon heard of this, he had the French Treasury Minister, Francois Barbe-Marabois offer to sell the entire Louisiana Territory to the Americans for $15 million. Though this offer exceeded their authority, Monroe and Livingston jumped

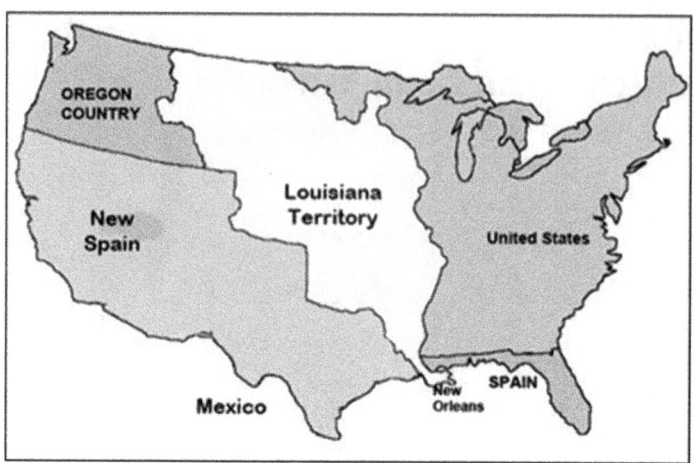

Fig. 8.1 North America in 1803. *Source* Fradin (2010)

at the opportunity to buy the entire Louisiana Territory, and after getting Jefferson's approval, they negotiated a deal with the French that was finally sealed on December 20, 1803.[1]

The purchase of the Louisiana Territory by the United States was one of the most remarkable real estate deals ever transacted, and it was a clear example of imperialism. With the stroke of a pen and a promise to pay the French $15 million, the Americans doubled the size of their country and made sure that New Orleans would remain in American hands. For his part, Napoleon got the money he needed for his European wars with Britain. As might be expected of a transaction of this magnitude, there was considerable debate over the terms of the transaction in the U.S. Congress. Jefferson's opponents in the Federalist Party—particularly those in the northeastern states—objected to the purchase, worrying that the expansion of agriculture in the southeastern United States would compete with their exports and would greatly expand the area of slave agriculture. The financial magnitude of the transaction was another concern. To cover the cost of the transaction the U.S. Government had to pay the French $3.75 million in cash and issue bonds at 6 percent interest to raise the balance of the debt. Ironically the bonds were taken by a Barings, a British Bank.

Once the deal was completed, the Louisiana Territory was under the control of the American Government. Though it would be several decades before a significant number Americans would start moving into the additional western territory, when they did come, they eagerly set up their farms and displaced anyone in their way. In his study of the westward march to the Pacific, historian Michael Golay describes his view of the characteristics of a typical settler moving into the Louisiana Territory:

> The Westering Americans were at once idealistic, greedy, visionary, solipsistic. They played for high stakes. They were builders, just as certainly, they were destroyers. I admire their dash their creative intensity, and their mother wit even as I deplore the destructive consequences, unlooked-for and otherwise, of their deeds and good intentions. (Golay, 2003, 13).

8.2 The Indian Removal Act

In 1803 most of the Louisiana Territory was home for Native American Nations, who did not welcome the intrusion of American settlers onto their land. In May of 1830 congress made it easier to for settlers to get land in the new territory by passing the Indian Removal Act. The act stipulated that Native Americans living in the Louisiana Territory could be forced to exchange their current property for land further west in the areas of Oklahoma and Kansas. In other words, Native Americans would have to move West. Prospective farmers in the eastern United States lost no time implementing the act to purchase the land for farms in the western United States. As historian Amy Greenberg notes, "Those who could not afford to buy land simply occupied it. These squatters as they were known repeatedly infringed on the property of Indian people."[2]

Between 1830 and 1850 more than 60,000 native Americans who lived on land acquired by the Louisiana Purchase had been removed from their homelands in the Southeast and sent to "Indian Country."[3] Each Indian nation was coerced into making an arrangement with the U.S. Government that opened their homeland to development by American settlers from the east. The process of moving them involved a brutal experience that became known as the "trail of tears." Suddenly pushed from their homes, travelers died of disease, exposure, and starvation on their way to their new homes in the Indian country of Oklahoma and Kansas.[4]

Most historians do not treat the forced removal of Native Americans to settlement of land in the Louisiana Territory by settlers from the east as an example of "imperial expansion." Yet, viewed from the perspective of those who had to give up claims to land they had inhabited for generations, the forced removal of Native Americans in the 1830s through the 1850s could hardly be viewed as anything else. Imperialism involves the forced acquisition or control of new territories. The Indian Removal Act encouraged both acquisition and control of a vast territory of land, and it was supported by a doctrine that became known as *Manifest Destiny*. Supporters of Manifest Destiny argued that the expansion of the United States across the entire American continent was a god given right that was an essential element in the growth of the American Republic.[5]

By the late 1830s the Spanish Empire was falling apart, and Americans were eager to take advantage of the collapse to increase the size of the United States. In 1819 Spain and the United States signed the Onis Adams Treaty, after years of negotiation to acquire Florida. The Americans had insisted that this territory was part of the Louisiana Purchase. Spain finally agreed to cede Florida to the United States for a mere $5 million.[6] The United States now controlled an unbroken coastline from Northern Maine to New Orleans and the Mississippi River.

8.3 Slavery and Annexation

On March 2, 1836, the Mexican province of Texas declared its independence from the Republic of Mexico and established itself as the Republic of Texas. What followed was a series of bitterly fought battles; the most famous of which was the Mexican triumph at the Alamo on March 6, 1836. However, the Mexican advantage was short-lived. On April 21 the Texian Army under Sam Houston managed to surprise and defeat a much larger Mexican Army commanded by Mexican President Antonio Lopez de Santa Anna at the battle of San Jacinto. Accounts of the battle vary, but Americans estimated that the number of Mexicans killed exceeded 500, while Texian losses were 9 killed and 22 wounded.[7] One of the many prisoners taken by the Texians was the Mexican president, Santa Anna, who, in exchange for his eventual release, agreed to sign a document giving the Republic of Texas its independence.

Despite the success of their army, the Texians knew that their independence was, at best, a fragile victory. The Mexican government had refused to accept the agreement that Santa Anna had signed ending the fighting in 1836 since he was a prisoner of the Texians when he signed the document. The Republic of Texas was a small country wedged between two much larger rivals, the Mexican Republic and the United States, each of whom coveted the Texian's resources. Since most Texians were eager to escape a return to the Mexican Republic, the best option for their political future would seem to be annexation with the United States. There was considerable sentiment in the United States, fueled by proponents of the manifest destiny doctrine, in favor of annexation of Texas. However, there were two obstacles working against annexation. The first obstacle was the fear that annexation would almost certainly lead to a war with Mexico. Though most Americans probably believed that the United States could win such a conflict, the country was hardly prepared for a war, and there was a distinct lack of enthusiasm to fight a war with Mexico over the acquisition of Texas.

A more serious problem was the issue of slavery. Many of the Americans who had migrated to Texas were southerners who owned slaves, and they took their slaves with them when they moved to Texas and set up their farms. In 1829 the Mexican Republic had abolished slavery; an act that caused slave owners in Texas to support the creation of an independent country in order to live in a country where they could keep their slaves. However, adding another slave state to the American Union was not a simple matter. By the mid-1840s the issue of slavery had become a very touchy political issue in the United States. Adding a new slave state would threaten the delicate political balance of slave and free states.

8.4 The Introduction of Slavery to the United States

African slaves had been introduced to the British Colonies in America in the early eighteenth century. By the beginning of the nineteenth century the number of slaves—most of whom resided in the southern states—reached just under one million men, women, and children. In an effort to slow the growth of slavery—and hopefully to eliminate the system altogether—Congress made it illegal to import slaves in into the United States in 1807. However, shutting down the slave trade did little to slow growth of the slave population. Because slaves were encouraged to have families. the slave population of the United States grew as rapidly as the free white population. By the time of the 1840 Census, there were 2.5 million slaves in the United States. In 1821 the admission of Missouri, which was a slave state, had created a flurry of political concern over the balance of free and slave states until Maine was admitted to even the balance of states at eleven.[8] In subsequent years care was taken to maintain that balance. Only two new states—Arkansas in 1836 and Michigan in 1837—had been added by the time the Texians sought admission to the Union.

8.5 The Election of 1840 and William Henry Harrison's Death

Adding Texas as a new state had become a major political issue by the time of the 1840 presidential election. After a spirited convention the Whigs chose former general William Henry Harrison as their candidate for president and John Tyler of Virginia as his running mate. Harrison had made a name for himself as the man who killed the Indian chief Tecumseh in the battle of Tippecanoe. The Democrats stayed with the incumbent president, Martin Van Buren, and did not select anyone for vice president. With a battle cry of "Tippecanoe and Tyler Too!," Harrison and Tyler cruised to a fairly easy victory. Unfortunately, Harrison, who was 68 years old, died one month after taking office on March 14, 1841, and John Tyler became President.

While Harrison had been a moderate candidate on the issue of slavery and statehood for Texas, Tyler was a southern slaveholder who strongly favored western advancement and American statehood for the Republic of Texas. He recognized that in the tangled politics following the election of 1840 and Harrison's death, approval of statehood for Texas by both houses of Congress because of the slave issue was not very likely. However, Tyler refused to give up his efforts to bring Texas into the Union. There was a new issue emerging in the form of the growing efforts of Great Britain and France to establish links to Texas that would give the European powers a presence in the area south of the United States. Americans still had a deep distrust of the British. Annexation of Texas would block the European interference, so Tyler and other American diplomats turned their efforts to working out terms of a treaty that would annex the Republic of Texas to the United States as a new state. By early

1844 they had completed their work, and the proposed treaty agreement was sent to the U.S. Senate. Although it required only a majority vote to become law, on June 8, 1844, the treaty proposal was defeated 35 to 16.

That might have ended the Texas annexation issue, but 1844 was an election year.

8.6 Manifest Destiny and the Election of 1844

The Whigs and the Democrats met in the fall of 1844, to select their presidential candidates for the presidential election. American politics at this point were in considerable disarray because of the dispute over slavery, the debate over Texas and the push for Manifest Destiny. Whigs were strongly opposed to slavery and for that reason they were unenthusiastic about the possibility of Texas annexation. They were concentrated in the northern and some western states, and their support for western expansion focused on the possibility of getting California from Mexico without a war and peacefully settling the boundary dispute with Great Britain over the Oregon Territory. Southern Democrats strongly defended slavery and were therefore enthusiastic about admitting Texas.

President John Tyler had been elected vice president in 1840 and became president upon the death of William Henry Harrison. Harrison had campaigned on his fame as a general, and he had been careful to position himself as a moderate on the slave and Texas issues. Tyler was a slave holder from Virginia who strongly supported the admission of Texas. Shortly after he was sworn in as President Tyler bolted from the Whig Party; completely reorganized Harrison's cabinet; and announced that he would serve the remainder of his term without any party affiliation.

The Whigs held their presidential convention in Baltimore at the beginning of May 1844. They had won the 1840 presidential election handily, however the death of President Harrison and the defection of John Tyler meant that they needed a new candidate. They decided to nominate Henry Clay of Kentucky'. Clay was a long-time leader of the party, and the Whigs were confident that he could defeat any candidate that the Democrats might nominate.

The Democrats held their convention in Baltimore at the end of May. The annexation of Texas was one of the central policy issues discussed by the delegates. As an incumbent president Martin Van Buren was an obvious candidate for re-election, however, the ex-president was cool to the prospect of adding Texas and he was unable to muster a majority from the democrats at the convention. On the ninth ballot, the vote swung to James Polk of Tennessee, who was a protégé of former president Andrew Jackson, and an avid supporter of western expansion. Though the popular vote in the election was fairly close, Polk easily won the contest in the electoral college carrying 15 states with a vote of 170–105.

8.7 A "Joint Resolution" for Annexation of Texas

In the spring of 1845, Tyler, now a lame-duck president, was continuing his efforts to have Texas admitted to the Union. After much pushing and tugging of congressional coattails, he was able to construct what was termed a "Joint Resolution for annexing Texas to the United," that was sent to both houses of congress. The document stated that Texas could be admitted to the Union. President-elect Polk strongly supported the admission of Texas, and he backed this unusual procedure. The same congress that had soundly defeated statehood for Texas only a few months earlier approved Tyler's Resolution. The document was immediately sent to the Texas legislature for their approval, and the Texans accepted the offer. All that remained was the signature of the U.S. President, and on March 1, 1844, President John Tyler signed the resolution making Texas the 26th state of the Union, on the last day of his term as president of the United States.[9]

8.8 Polk's War

On March 5, 1844 James Polk took the oath of office to be president of the United States. Polk was the quintessential imperialist. He had campaigned on a platform of Manifest Destiny that not only included the annexation of Texas, but also looked for a way to acquire Alta California from Mexico and to obtain the Oregon territory from Great Britain. As soon as he was sworn in as President of the United States. Polk offered to buy California from Mexico for $25 million. When the Mexican government refused the offer, Polk decided that the only way he was likely to fulfill his territorial ambitions would be to start a war with Mexico. He ordered general Zachary Taylor, a veteran of the Indian wars whose nickname was "rough and ready," to take a force of 10,000 American soldiers to an area of west Texas that had been claimed by both Mexico and Texas, and was still a matter of dispute between the two countries. On April 25, 1846, a group of American soldiers ventured into the disputed territory and was attacked by Mexican cavalry. Eleven American soldiers were killed.

Polk had the excuse he needed for a war with Mexico. As soon as the news reached Washington D.C., the president asked Congress to declare war on Mexico; charging that "American blood": had been spilled on "American" soil. There is some question whether the American troops were actually on American soil when they were attacked by the Mexican forces. Historian Amy Greenberg takes note of an American soldier who wrote in a diary he kept that "We have not one particle of right to be here, it looks as if the government sent a small force on purpose to bring on a war, so as to have a pretext for taking California and as much of this country as it chooses."[10] Not all historians agree with Greenberg's claim that Congress accepted Polk's claim that the Mexican troops had actually violated American sovereignty, and hence her charge that this was a "wicked war" Jack Bauer takes a somewhat more accepting view of Polk's claim that the Americans were on "American soil" than Greenberg, since both Mexico and the United States claimed that part of Texas.[11] However historians felt about the issue of whether or not the American troops were on Mexican soil, President Polk got the war that he wanted; now what he needed to do was to turn his attention to winning that war. The president had devoted considerable time getting the war with Mexico started, but he had not bothered to pay a lot of attention to the details involving how to fight the war. On paper, at least, fighting a war with Mexico in the spring of 1846 appeared be a major challenge. The American Army at that time consisted of 637 officers and 5925 enlisted men—hardly enough to invade and conquer a country the size of Mexico. The Mexicans had a standing army of 18,000 men with another 10,000 men in reserve.[12]

The American army may have been small, but it could count on an impressive group of young officers, many of whom who were products of the Military Academy that Congress had established at West Point in 1803. Names such as Robert E. Lee, Ulysses Grant, William Tecumseh Sherman, Thomas Jackson, and Jubal Early are at the top of a long list of West Point graduates who fought as junior officers in the Mexican War. In addition to these men the army could count on a substantial body of young junior officers who had an elementary education and at least some military experience from fighting in the "Indian wars." Micheal Clodfelter estimates that: "a total of 78,718 regulars and volunteers served in Mexico and what was to become the American Southwest and 40,000 of them were in the field at the conflict's conclusion."[13]

8.9 Polk's Plan for the War

Polk had a simple plan for winning the war: American troops would immediately launch several invasions of Mexico and eventually occupy Mexico City. Figure 7.2 shows charts for the results of this series of battles between May of 1846 and the battle of Buena Vista in September 1848.

Although the Mexicans had a substantial edge in the number of men engaged in all but one of these early battles, they were all American victories. Where the Americans had a substantial advantage was in the way they used their artillery They had organized their artillery units to include what were known as "flying artillery" units that had small cannons which could quickly be moved from one spot to another to repel infantry charges with volleys of "canister." Every batttle had at least one instance where these artillery units contributed to anAmerican victory. Both sides suffered heavy casualties in the fighting; a reflection of the fierceness which this war was fought once the armies were engaged.

By the beginning of September American forces had gained reinforcements and Taylor was ready to move south in accordance with President's broad orders that the primary object of occupying the northern areas of Mexico was to have Mexico city as their principal objective.

8.10 The Battle of Buena Vista

The American Army was now prepared to move south to attack the Mexican forces at Buena Vista in central Mexico. In one of the largest battles of the war American troops forced the Mexicans to pull back towards Mexico City (See Fig. 7.3). Meanwhile, President Polk had appointed Winfield Scott as commander in chief for all of the American forces in Mexico, with orders to attack Mexico City as soon as possible. Scott assembled a force of around 18,000 men to arrive from New Orleans. He also built some "surfcrafts"—flat bottom boats—constructed that could be used for landing on beaches. On March 9th 1847 Scott's entire American force landed landed at a beach just south of Veracruz, Mexico without suffering any serious casualties. The Americans occupied the Fort protecting the city at Veracruz and wasted no time before advancing inland. On March 18th the Americans defeated a sizesable Mexican force at Cero Gordo before turning north towards Mexico City. The Mexicans put up a stout resistance before surrendering their capital city, but once Taylor's troops arrived from the north, Scott's army was able to subdue the three main forts protecting Mexico City. Cero Gordo, Conteras/Charubusco, and Chathederal City—were eventually forced to surrender in some of the most serious fighting of the war, and the data on casualties in Fig. 8.2. On September 14th General Scott—entered Mexico City and the Mexican Government agreed to end the war (Fig. 8.3).

8.11 The Trteaty of Guadalupe Hidalgo

The Trteaty of Guadalupe Hidalgo ended the fighting between the United States and Mexico. With American troops parading through Mexico City, the American experiment with imperialism was becoming exactly what President Polk wanted: one of the most successful imperial ventures in the nineteenth century. The war had accomplished exactly what President Polk wanted. Mexico agreed to cede a grant of land to the United States that included the present-day states of California, Nevada, Utah, significant parts of Colorado, New Mexico, and Arizona, and a small portion of Wyoming. Manifest destiny had been realized, and the United States had joined the list of countries exercising some form of imperial power.

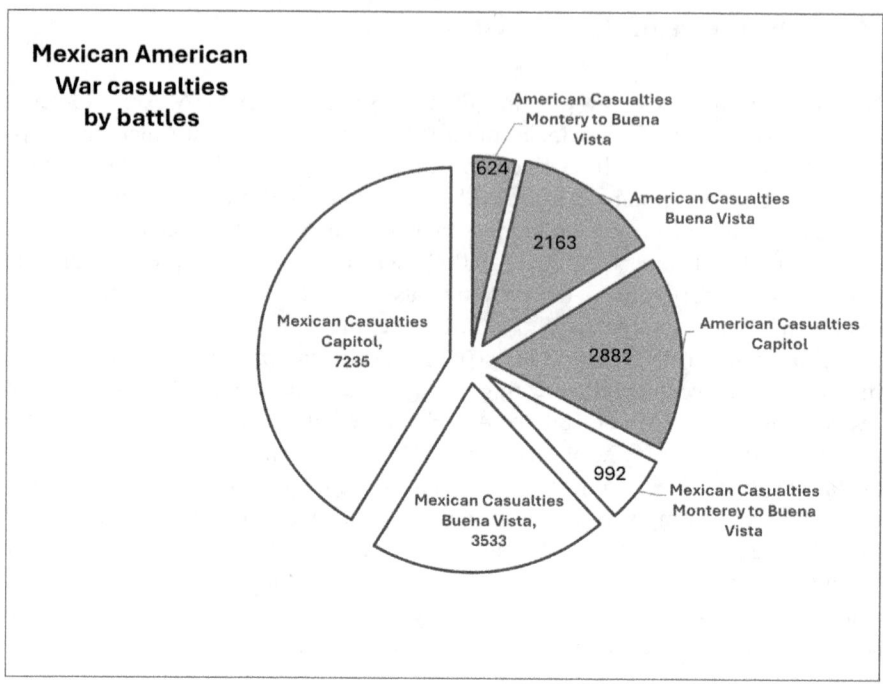

Fig. 8.2 Mexican American war casualties. *Sources* Clodfelter (2015), Greenberg (2012), Merry (2009) and Winders (2002)

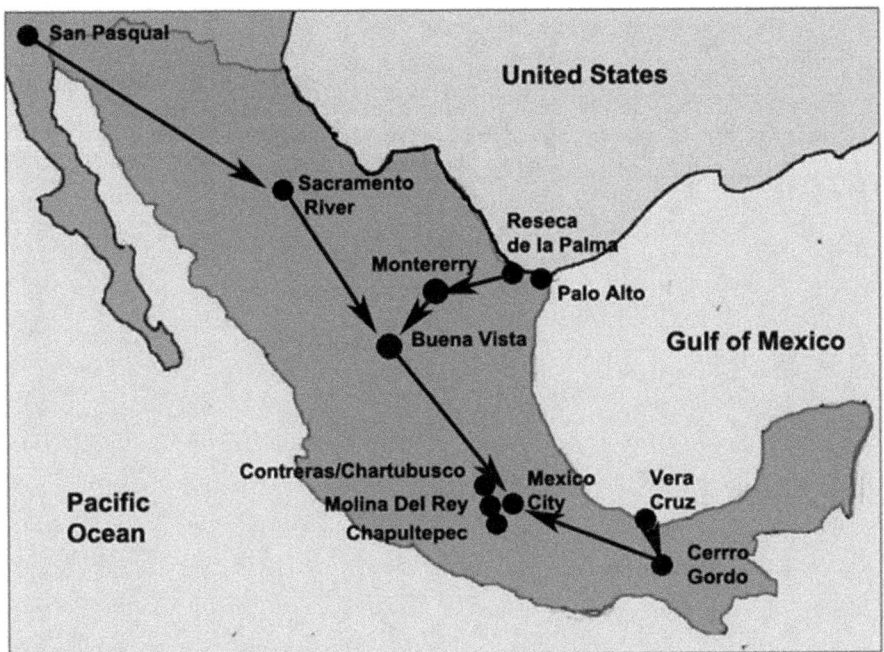

Fig. 8.3 The Mexican American war-battles. *Sources* Clodfelter (2015), Greenberg (2012), Merry (2009) and Winders (2002)

Notes

1. For more on the political controversies surrounding the Louisiana Purchase see Merk (1966), Golay (2003), and Fradin (2010).
2. Greenberg (2012, 10).
3. The Five Civilized Indian tribes were the Cherrokee the Muscogee the Seminole the Chickasaw and the Choctaw Nations.
4. There is an extensive literature on the removal of Indian tribes to the West and the horrors of forced removal along the Trail of Tears. See Brown (2007), Greenberg (2012) and Golay (2003).
5. For more on the religious and ideological support for manifest destiny see Greenberg (2012).
6. Merk (1963, 15.)
7. For accounts of the battle and the number of casualties see Clodfelter (2002), Winders (2002), and Merry (2009).
8. The "balance" involved in this equation was not the number of states; it was the balance in the number of senators from each state in the U.S. Congress. The founding fathers had designed this balance to protect small states from being dominated by large states. By 1820 the relevant division was states that allowed slavery versus states that allowed it.

9. Texas was the only state which achieved statehood by this procedure of "annexation" of a independent state.
10. Greenberg (2012, 103) As the title of her book suggests, Greenberg feels that the conflict was a "wicked war" that was deliberately started by a lie on the part of President Polk.
11. For a more detailed account of Polk's maneuvering with Congress, see Bauer (1974).
12. The estimate of Mexican troops is from Newell (2014, 8).
13. Clodfelter (2002).

Chapter 9
The American Civil War

The Treaty of Guadalupe Hidalgo settled the issue of manifest destiny between the United States and Mexico for the time being, but it did nothing to reduce the growing conflict within the United States over the system of slavery in the southern states. A series of laws that became known as the Compromise of 1850 included a provision that California was would be admitted into the Union as a "free" state. The Compromise also provided a condition that the new state governments that would be established in the territory obtained from Mexico would be free to choose whether or not these new states could allow slavery. A Fugitive Slave Act was passed that made it easier for slave owners to claim runaway slaves as their property, even if they had managed to flee to the North. Finally, slavery was abolished in Washington D.C.

Unfortunately, all of these efforts failed to come up with a compromise that would satisfy southern slaveholders. Early on the morning of April 12, 1861, soldiers of the South Carolina state militia began a bombardment of Union Soldiers in Fort Sumter, which was located in the center of Charleston harbor. After a full day of bombardment, the Union troops surrendered. President Lincoln could not ignore the military action; the bombardment of Fort Sumter became the first military action of a war that lasted for just over 4 years of bitter fighting.[1]

9.1 Abraham Lincoln as the Imperialist

American Historians do not usually refer to this this war as an "imperial" war; it is usually just referred to as the American Civil War. However, if we step back and look at the conflict from the perspective of a southern slaveholder in 1861, it certainly has all the characteristics of an imperial war. Lincoln's election in the 1860 election gave the Republican party what seemed to be an ironclad monopoly in the government of the United States. At the head of that government was an imperialist who was committed to placing limits on the expansion of slavery, and who stated in a speech in 1858 that

> We are now far into the fifth year, since a policy was initiated, with the avowed and *confident* promise, of putting an end to slavery agitation. Under the operation of that policy, that agitation has not only *not ceased*, but has *constantly augmented*. In *my* opinion, it *will* not cease, until a *crisis* shall have been reached, and passed *A house divided against itself cannot stand*.[2]

Southern slaveholders did not take issue with Lincoln's claim that a house divided could not stand. However, Lincoln went on to explain that he believed that:

> This government cannot endure, permanently half *slave* and half *free*. I do not expect the Union to be *dissolved* - I do not expect the house to *fall*- but I do expect it will cease to be divided. It will become *all* one thing, or *all* the other.[3]

There was no doubt in the mind of any slaveholder that Lincoln's long-term objective was to rid the country of what he considered an abominable system of slavery. Not surprisingly, when the returns of the election of 1860 came in and it became clear that Lincoln was going to be an imperialist president, Southerners realized that they had no choice to either accept the emancipation of slavery in the South or leave the Union.

9.2 Secession and the Civil War

It was not a hard choice to make. Slaves and cotton were a central part of southern agriculture in the middle of the nineteenth century. The capital invested by slaveholders represented roughly one half of all capital investment in the Confederacy.[4] Northern imperialists were threatening to take that capital away from slaveholders with without any compensation in the spring of 1861, and Southern slaveholders viewed the threat of emancipation of slaves as an act of outright imperialism on the part of Republicans. By the time of Lincoln's inauguration on March 4, 1861, seven states had seceded from the Union.[5] Eventually, four more states left the Union to form the Confederate States of America. At least 750,000 northern and southern soldiers died in the American Civil War, making it the deadliest war anywhere in the world between the Battle of Waterloo in 1814 and the battles of the First World War.[6]

The northern states fought the war to preserve the Union. They had a huge advantage in terms of the number of men to serve in their armies and a manufacturing sector that could supply their troops. The Southerners fought to maintain a system of slave labor that proved to be extraordinarily efficient at producing cotton. The southerners were able to stay with the Northern Forces until the two armies met outside the small town of Gettysburg Pennsylvania over a weekend in July 1863. Late in the afternoon of July 3rd Robert E Lee, the commander of the Confederate forces, ordered the 12,000 men in General George Pickett's division to charge into the center of the Union lines in an effort to break through and win the battle. Unfortunately for the rebels, Pickett's charge failed, and Lee and his army were forced to retreat back to Virginia.

Gettysburg was the last real chance that the Confederates had to win the war. In the same weekend that they lost the battle of Gettysburg, Confederate troops in the city of Vicksburg, Mississippi surrendered to the union troops surrounding their city. The Confederacy could not survive the losses at both Gettysburg and Vicksburg. The war went on for another year, but on April 9, 1865 Lee surrendered to the head of the Union General, Ulysses Grant, at Appomattox, Virginia ending the war.

The American Civil War was one of the most important imperial wars of the nineteenth century. The success of the Northern armies in keeping the United States together had profound implications for the future stability of the world. By the end of nineteenth century the United States had come together as the most powerful nation in the world, and an imperial nation in its own right.

9.3 Emancipation and the South After the Civil War

The Northern victory also had profound changes within the United States. With the southern representatives no longer in Congress, the 13th amendment was added to the constitution. The wording was simple and right to the issue in question:

> Neither slavery nor involuntary servitude, except as a punishment for crime where of the party shall have been duly convicted, shall exist within the United States, or any place subject to their jurisdiction.

The right to own slaves simply disappeared. Both the planters and the freed slaves had to find new ways to incorporate the free blacks into the agricultural system so that they could continue to grow cotton, tobacco, and sugar together with a variety of other crops to feed the families and farm animals.

Ex-slaves had no financial assets, and they were not eager to work as field hands. However, they had few choices, and it would take some time to construct a new tenure system. Reconstruction was not a simple process. What slowly emerged was a complex system of land tenure that allowed both blacks and whites to work on family farms with a variety of tenure arrangements.

A few features of the new tenure system indicate the extent of the changes.

1. By 1880 the plantation system had virtually died out. Fewer than one percent of cotton farms were still in operation. There were some other large farms, but the total fraction of lightly above 5 percent.
2. The largest change was the reliance on small family farms where most of the labor was done by the farmer and his family. About half of these farms were owned by the farmer.
3. About one third of all farms worked on a system known as sharecropping. In this case the farmer gave a share of his cotton to the farmer or merchant to pay for his supplies.

Reconstruction—the programs passed by Congress to admit the Confederate states back into the Union—was largely completed by 1900. The slaves were freed, and as Ransom and Sutch note in their study of Emancipation:

On November 18, 1865 Abraham Lincoln visited Gettysburg to visit a ceremony to bury the Union soldiers who died in the battle. In his short speech the President remarked that "The world will little note, nor long remember what we say here, but it can never forget what they did here." He was only partially correct; the world did remember what he said: "this nation, under God, shall have a new birth of freedom—and that government of the people, by the people, for the people, shall not perish from the earth."

Lincoln did not live long enough to enjoy his imperial victory. He was assassinated by southern secessionist John Wilkes Booth on April 14, 1865; less than a week after Robert E. Lee had surrendered to end the war at Appomattox Virginia.

The victory of the Northern Imperialists ended slavery in United states. It was one of the few instances where imperialists were successful in their efforts to use an imperial war to impose a major change of the political structure of the country resisting change.

Notes

1. There is a huge library of books and other publications on the American Civil War. On the War Among the best single volumes are those by James McPherson (1988, 2003). For more on the war as a revolutionary war see Ransom and Sutch (2001).
2. The quote is taken from Lincoln's speech was taken from a cite in Wikipedia.
3. The quote is taken from Lincoln's speech was taken from a cite in Wikipedia.
4. The total value of slaves in the South is from Ransom and Sutch (1988).
5. The states that seceded were South Carolina, Mississippi, Florida, Alabama, Georgia, Louisiana, and Texas.
6. There is some question about the total number of the deaths in the American Civil War. For many years, the accepted number of total deaths men killed in battle has been 620,000. However, this estimate reflects the battle deaths reported at the time of the battle. J. David Hacker has used data from the deaths reported in the 1870 census to show that the battle deaths from both sides in the war must have totaled at least 750,000 men. See Hacker (2011).

Chapter 10
The Crimean War

10.1 A Fool's Charge

The Crimean War, which was fought between an alliance of Britain, France, and Turkey in an effort to check the imperial advance of Russia is best remembered because of a poem written by the British poet Alfred, Lord *Tennyson*,[1] describing the disastrous c*harge of 600 troops of a British light cavalry* unit at the Battle of Balaclava:

> Half a league, half a league,
> Half a league onward,
> All in the valley of Death
> Rode the six hundred.
> "Forward, the Light Brigade!
> Charge for the guns!" he said:
> Into the valley of Death
> Rode the six hundred.
>
> "Forward, the Light Brigade!"
> Was there a man dismay'd?
> Not tho' the soldier knew
> Some one had blunder'd:
> Theirs not to make reply,
> Theirs not to reason why,
> Theirs but to do and die:
> Into the valley of Death
> Rode the six hundred.

> Cannon to right of them,
> Cannon to left of them,
> Cannon in front of them
> Volley'd and thunder'd;
> Storm'd at with shot and shell,
> Boldly they rode and well,
> Into the jaws of Death,
> Into the mouth of Hell
> Rode the six hundred.

Alfred Lord Tennyson's poem, which was widely popular at the time, captured the bravery of British troops who blindly obeyed their orders to charge, and it also suggested that the technology of warfare had become more deadly. Of the 600 cavalry men in the light brigade who started the charge. 110 men were killed and another 110 were wounded.[2]

The Crimean war was the first significant conflict between European imperial powers since Napoleon's defeat at Waterloo nearly 30 years earlier. The War started on March 28, 1854, when Great Britain and France declared war on Russia. The two countries were concerned that the Russians were threatening what was left of the Ottoman Empire in an effort to increase their influence in the area around the Black Sea.

Figure 10.1 shows the major battles of the war. The British and the French gathered an army of just over 50,000 troops in Constantinople and ferried them to Varna in September 1854 on the west coast of the Black Sea. From there they planned to move to Russia and attacked the Russian port of Sevastopol. The Russians managed to block the Allied advance at Battle of Inkerman, on November 5, and the Allies established a siege of the city which lasted until September 1855. With the siege lifted the Allies started to move north to invade Russia, building a railroad on the way.

By this time both the Russians and the British-French allies were getting tired of a war that was rapidly turning into a stalemate. Both sides were looking for a way to settle their differences. The war had taken an enormous toll of death on both sides. Table 10.1 shows the number of casualties and the number of men who died from sickness.

The British and the French had managed to check the efforts of the Russians to extend their territory South and control the Ottoman Empire. It was a high price to pay to simply maintain the status quo in the Imperial tug-of-war that was the Middle East at the middle of the nineteenth century.

Notes

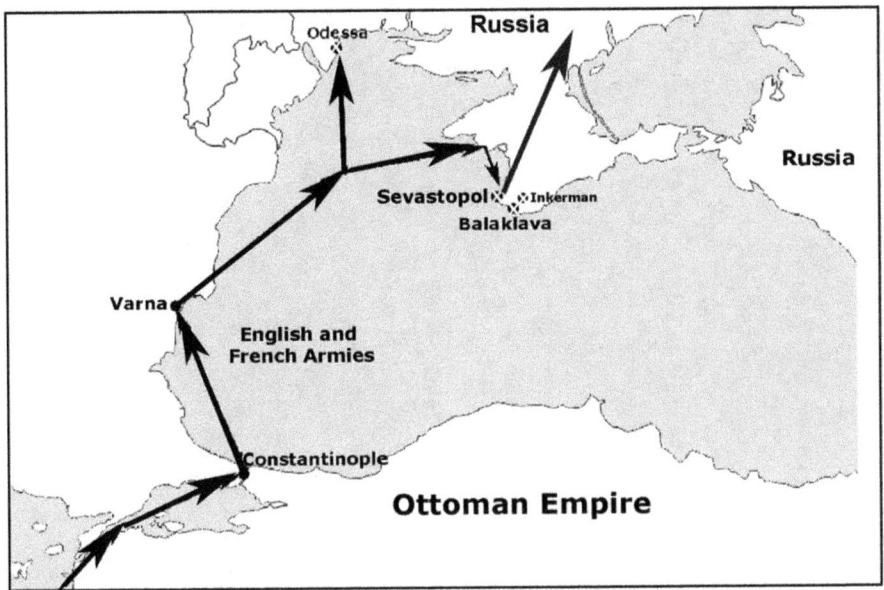

Fig. 10.1 The Crimean war. *Source* Clodfleter (2015)

Table 10.1 Casualties in the Crimean war

Country	Men mobilized	Killed in action	Died of illness	Total deaths	Percent deaths
Great Britain	97,864	4602	17,580	22,182	22.7
France	309,268	20,240	75,375	95,615	30.9
Ottoman	165,000	20,000	24,500	44,500	26.9
Total	572,132	44,842	117,455	162,297	28.4
Russia	324,478	73,125	75,375	148,500	45.8

The estimates deaths are from Clodfelter (2002, 283)

Notes

1. The quote of Lord Alfred Tennyson's Poem is from *Wikipedia*.
2. The estimate of casualties suffered by the Light Brigade is from Clodfelter (2002, 203).

Chapter 11
CINC: A Measure of Military Capability

In the days of Hernan Cortez and Francisco Pizzaro soldiers owned their own weapons, which usually consisted of a heavy sword along with steel plated amor. They served in well-trained units of regiments and brigades that could be called to action when needed. Some of the infantry units would be armed with muskets that had a maximum range of 100 yards and it took several moments to reload the muskets before another volley could be fired. Infantry units might be also accompanied by artillery units, however, fighting battles in the fifteenth century would eventually come down to hand-to-hand melees that went on until one side or the other chose to withdraw.

11.1 War, Economics, and the Gunpowder Revolution

By the middle of the nineteenth century things had changed dramatically. The clumsy muskets had been replaced by French Chassepot rifles that could fire repeating cartridges that could reach range of up to 1500 m. The Germans had developed cannons that were mobile and could reach targets that were out of sight. Armies became much more mobile with the introductions of railroads allowing for quicker and more sophisticated logistics and the battlefields much bigger as new weapons like canister shot came into use. The days when one could estimate an adversary's ability to fight a war by simply counting how many soldiers they could have in action for a battle were gone.

The gunpowder revolution had created a world where military ability was measured not only by a state's ability to field men who could fight; what mattered was whether they could supply their army with the improved weapons that came along with the introduction of gunpowder that changed the nature of battles. All this made the task of military planners who had to judge a prospective adversary's ability to wage a war more difficult. It also makes the task of military historians trying to explain how some country managed to win a war more difficult. In 1963 J. David Singer, a professor of political science at the University Michigan, founded the *Correlates of War Project* at the University of Michigan. One of Singers' first projects was to work out a statistical method for judging the strength of a country's military power. He produced a statistic which he called the *Composite Index of Military Capability—CINC*.

The CINC combines data from six variables that measure the military, economic, and demographic preparedness of a country to wage war. The variables are:

Military Features

MILEX = Military Expenditures in British Pound Sterling
MILPER = Number of Individuals in the Military

Economic Features

ISTR = Tons of Iron and Steel Produce
PEC = Level of Energy Consumption

Demographic Features

TOTPOP = Total Population
UPOP = Urban Population

These variables are expressed as a ratio of the world's total production of that variable:
The CINC can then be computed as:

CINC = (MILEX + MILPER + ISTR + PEC + TOTPOP + UPOP)/6

The Correlates of War Project has computed the CINC for 193 states, in some cases dating back as far as 1816. In addition to providing a measure of the CINC, the Project provides measures for each of the six variables along with extensive data on wars. This data will form the basis for much of our analysis of the imperial wars from 1450 to 1945.[1]

Note

1. For more on Singer's work and the Correlates of War see Singer (1972).

Chapter 12
Bismark's Wars

12.1 Otto Von Bismark, the Imperialist

In the spring of 1862, King Wilhelm I of Prussia was having difficulties getting his budget approved by the Prussian Landtag. In an effort to resolve the issue, he appointed Otto von Bismarck as the Minister President of Prussia. It turned out to be a brilliant decision. Bismark not only got the budget quickly approved; together with Wilhelm he remained at the head of the Prussian government—and later the German Empire—for the next 28 years.

Otto von Bismark was a man who did not believe in long parliamentary debates before acting. Shortly after he took office in 1862, he gave a speech to the Landtag assuring them that: "it is not by speeches and majority resolutions that the great questions of the time are decided—that was the big mistake of 1848 and 1849—but by iron and blood."[1] The main objective of his foreign policy was to unite the 39 states of the German Federation into a German Empire with Wilhelm I as Emperor of the new regime and Prussia as the dominant power in the new government with a policy of iron and blood. His role in turning the German state of Prussia of 1862 into the German Empire of 1871 ranks among the most successful imperialist wars of the nineteenth century.

Bismark started his first war shortly after he became President of Prussia. There had been a prolonged disturbance between the Duchies of Schleswig,—Prussia, Austria-Hungary, and Denmark. Bismark was determined to end the disturbance and bring both Dutchies under the control of Prussia. The Prussians and Austrians joined forces long enough to defeat Denmark in two short wars that established control of the German duchies of Holstein and Lauenburg, together the ethnically mixed Danish duchy of Schleswig.

12.2 The Seven Weeks War Between Austria and Prussia

The union of the two German states armies did not last for long. Bismark, together with his minister of war, Albrecht Roon, and his chief of Staff. Helmuth von Moltke, were determined to see that Prussia would eventually become the dominant state in the German Federation. On June 14, 1866, Prussia declared war on Austria. What became known as the *Seven Weeks War* ended on July 3, 1866 when the Prussian Army gained a decisive victory at the *Battle of Königgrätz*. The Treaty of Prague ended the war, and reorganized the German Federation. Five states formed a new North German Federation which had a military Alliance with Prussia. Austria was now out of the way, so the only state left that could challenge Prussia for leadership of Europe was France. While the Germans were reorganizing their states, the French had established a new state with Napoleon's nephew, Napoleon III as the Emperor of what became known as the Second Empire. It became increasingly obvious that these two states would eventually have to fight each other for the dominance of Europe.[2]

Both Prussia and France were ready for war by 1870. All they needed was an excuse to start fighting. That came in the form of a dispute over the Spanish throne in November 1869. The throne of Spain was vacant, and the Spanish government had offered it to Leopold de Hohenzollern, who was a Prussian prince. The French were not keen on having a Prussian Prince accept the Spanish Throne, and when Bismark managed to convince the French that he might be serious about endorsing Leopold, Louis Napoleon decided to take the bull by the horn and declare war against Prussia on June 16, 1870.

Bismark and Napoleon III had managed to find a way to start their Imperial war.

12.3 The Franco-Prussian War: Opening Moves

The French were able to mobilize 500,000 troops at the start of the war, and eventually Napoleon III was able put just over 2 million men into action during the war. French infantry were equipped with the new breech-loading Chassepot rifle, which had an effective range of 1600 m, which was well beyond the range of any other rifle at the time. The Chassepot gave French infantry a significant advantage and Louis Napoleon's generals were confident that with this new gun the French Army could defeat the Prussians. However, the French did not have any plans with which to begin hostilities. The absence of such plans, together with organizational failures of the French high command was a major factor in the ultimate defeat of French forces in this rather short war.

For their part, Roon, von Molte, and his fellow generals had been planning for a war with the French for several years. Like the French, they had made advances in their weapons, particularly with regard to their artillery. The Krup C-64 breech-loaded 4 pounder was a mobile and accurate field cannon hat was vastly superior to any of the artillery that the French could put into action. Bismark and von Moltke managed to mobilize 700,000 men at the start of the war; eventually 1.5 million German men fought in the war.[3] The Prussians had 11 artillery regiments, each equipped with six C-64 guns. Like the flying artillery units used by American armies in the Mexican American War, the Prussians were able to move their guns quickly and effectively. And the C-64 cannons proved to be very effective to deal with French infantry attacks because they could fire shells for a distance of 3000 yards and the shells exploded on contact. French infantry were unable to hold their ground against a concentrated Prussian artillery attack.

12.4 The Franco-Prussian War

By July 31st both armies were located near the French border and ready to fight. The French Armies, totaling 215,000 men, were commanded by Napoleon himself. This did not bode well for the French. Napoleon had proven himself to be a rather poor general when fighting the Italians a few years earlier, and he was now suffering from a severe case of kidney stones that seriously interfered with his ability to command troops on the battlefield. The first battles of the war favored the German forces as they attacked the French. Patrice MacMahon, the French commander, sent an initial report to Napoleon III that "I have lost the battle: we have suffered great losses in men and material; the retreat is at present in progress. I shall try to reach the point where I shall organize the Army" [4](Chrastil (2023, 71).

General MacMahon's message marked the beginning of a disastrous series of defeats for the French. Battles at Metz, Verdun, and Chalon. The Prussians gradually pushed the French armies into the town of Sedan, where the German forces were able to surround a French force of 104,000 troops, including MacMahon and Napoleon III. On September 2, 1871 Napoleon III surrendered; thus, ending the first phase of the war.

Figure 12.1 shows the Prussian invasion routes of Northern France. The ease with which the Prussian armies defeated French forces in northern France took the Prussians by surprise and produced a situation where von Moltke and his commanders could seriously consider an invasion of the rest of France. With Napoleon III and General MacMahon in captivity and the rest of the French Armies in total disarray, the Prussians began the invasion of France. By this time, the use of railroads had become an important part of the Prussian military plans. Moltke put his engineers to work extending railroads in order to move troops around more quickly, and the result was that all of northern France was occupied by Prussians by the end of September 1870. Figure 12.1 shows the battles in northern France that eventually allowed the Prussians to reach Paris and begin a siege of the city on September 19th. The Parisians finally surrendered on January 28, 1871, and the two sides agreed to an armistice that ended the fighting throughout France. However, talks of a peace settlement still faced serious obstacles. The French had set up a Government of National Defense and established the Third Republic at the beginning of September. However, the political chaos in French politics made any progress on peace conditions difficult

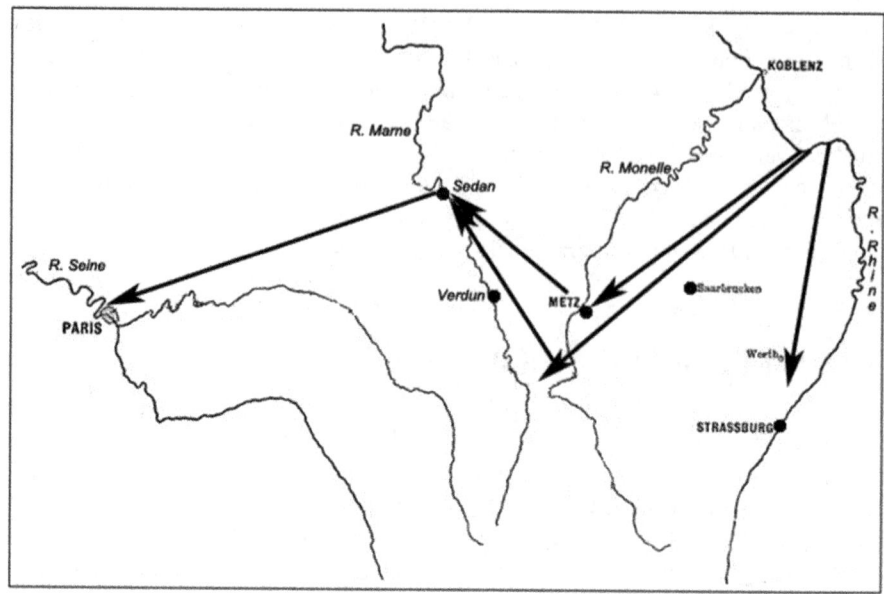

Fig. 12.1 The Prussian invasion of France, 1870. *Source* Chrastil (2023)

because the Prussians never knew who to talk to. Further complicating things was the announcement on December 16th that the Federation of North German States had been dissolved and that a new German Empire had been created with the Prussian King as the new Emperor.

12.5 A Treaty at Last

What finally emerged from the fighting was the Treaty of Frankfurt, which both sides signed on May 10, 1871, ending the war. The conditions of the treaty were straightforward:

- The French Recognized Wilhelm I as Emperor of the German Empire
- The treaty recognized the new border between France and the German Empire
- The French were forced to give up Alsace-Lorraine.
- France paid Germany five billion francs in reparations

The Franco-Prussian war had an enormous impact on the military future of the States in Europe. The German Empire that was created by Prussia's victory in the war was almost twice the size of Prussia before the war, and it had suddenly become the most powerful state in Europe. France, on the other hand, lingered in political and military obscurity for the next 40 years. Otto von Bismarck, with his "iron and blood" approach to politics, was able to play a dominant role in shaping the complex pattern

12.5 A Treaty at Last

Fig. 12.2 The impact of the Franco-Prussian war. *Source* Chrastil (2023)

of international treaties between states that ultimately led to the outbreak of the First World War in 1914 (Figs. 12.2, 12.3).

Through the 1850s Prussia's %CINC had stayed right around 5 percent. In 1870 it suddenly jumped to 10.6 percent as a result of the victory in the war with France. Bismark managed to keep the newly formed German Empire at that level of military readiness until his retirement in 1881. A further glance at the numbers in Table 12.1 reveals that all six of the variables in the %CINC calculation show a remarkable increase. A major part of the expansion of the German Empire came from the union of Prussia and the South German Federation in 1871 into the German Empire. However, what was also important to Prussia's rise to military dominance was Bismark's success maintaining the level of military expenditures and military personnel that did not go away after the end of the war. The impact of these changes in the relative strength of the German Empire can be seen in Fig. 11.3. In 1890 The German Empire had increased its CINC, while the CINC going to the Austrian Empire had experienced a sharp decline, while the %CINC going to the future Entente Countries has also declined.

Bismark's policies had put the German Empire in a position to challenge the Triple Entente; a situation that would continue to 1914 and the eve of the First World War.

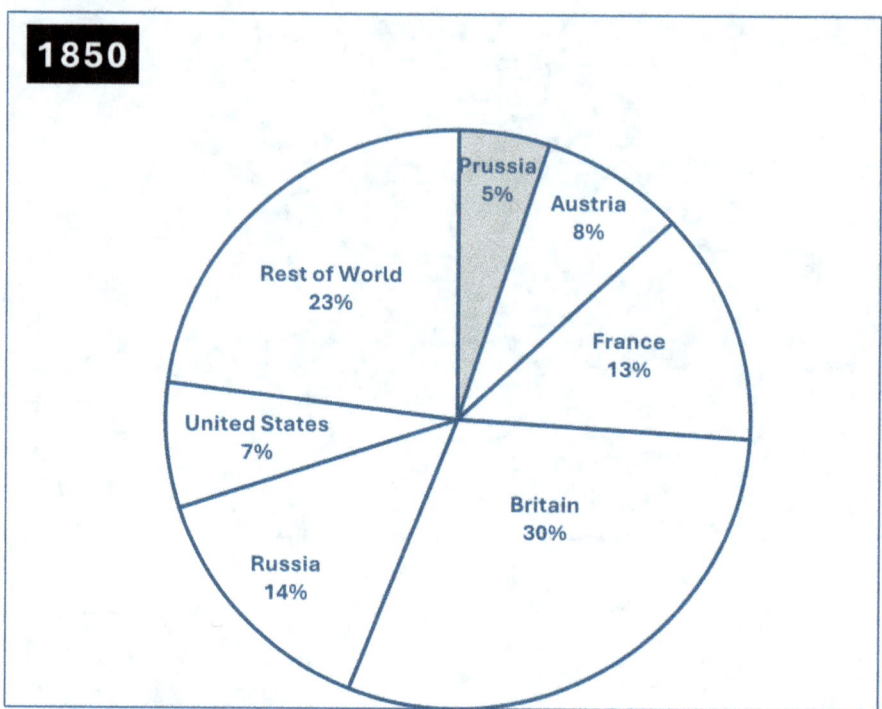

Fig. 12.3 Pie charts showing CINC of Germany 1850–1870. *Source* Singer and the correlates of war project https://correlatesofwar.org/

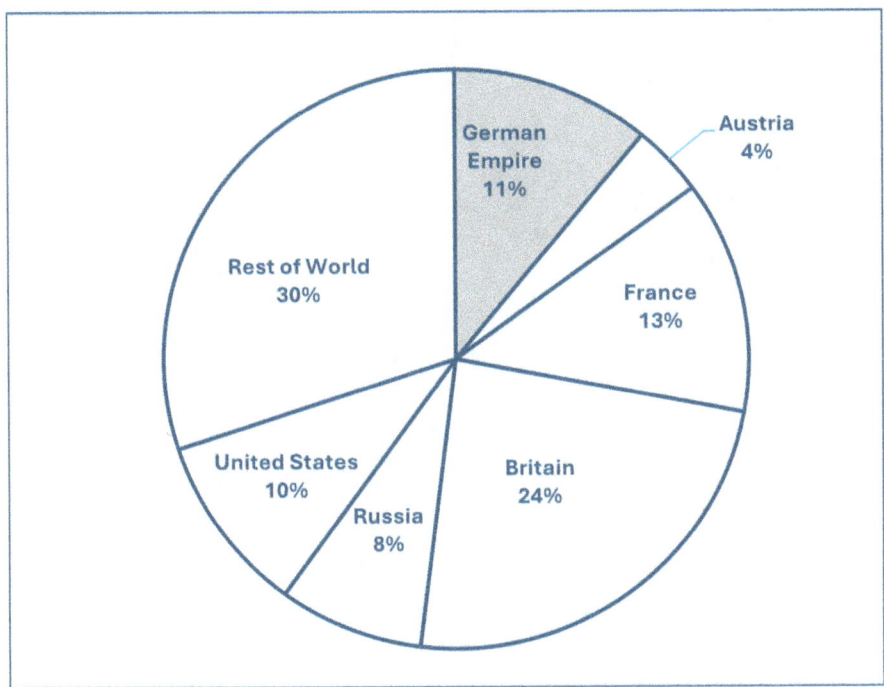

Fig. 12.3 (continued)

Table 12.1 Prussia and the German empire's %CINC—1850–1880

Year	MILEX	MILPER	ISTR	PEC	TOTPOP	UPOP	%CINC
1850	211	3528	131	5750	16,608	567	4.90
1855	317	3954	142	11,070	17,203	681	4.80
1860	490	4579	201	15,040	18,265	745	5.15
1865	988	5950	216	23,857	20,421	1020	6.48
1870	1261	42,993	319	28,817	31,194	1707	10.60
1875	1759	18,262	428	38,160	42,510	2471	10.34
1880	2468	19,397	430	47,298	45,093	3142	10.56

Notes

1. The quote was from a speech to the German Landtag on September 30, 1862.
2. Our discussion of the Prussian-Austrian rivalry and the Franco-Prussian war relies on Howard (2021), Chrastil (2023,) and Breuilly (1993), together with Clodfelter (2002).
3. The mobilization figures are from Clodfelter (2002, 208).
4. (Chrastil (2023, 71).

Chapter 13
The Spanish American War

On February 15, 1898, the USS Maine exploded in Havana Harbor. The morning edition of *The New York World* newspaper shouted the news for all to read:

13.1 The United States Declares War on Spain

Although the newspapers—and the American Government—were quick to blame the Spanish Government for the explosion, the true cause of the blast remains a mystery despite numerous efforts by numerous investigations which have suggested that the most likely explanation was that it was an explosion of ammunition stored in the bow of the ship. However, Congress and President William McKinley remained convinced that the Spanish were involved in the battleship explosion, and on April 25, 1898, the President asked Congress to declare war on Spain. Whatever the correct explanation for the explosion on the *Maine*, it touched off a war between the United States and Spain.

It did not take long for the American Navy to react to the declaration of war. On May 1 Commodore George Dewey and a squadron of American ships attacked a Spanish fleet that was at anchor in Manila Bay. The Americans sank all ten Spanish ships in the battle without any American ships getting damaged. This encounter was followed by a second battle between the two navies on July 3rd at Santiago Harbor, Cuba. where a squadron of American ships sank four Spanish armored cruisers and two destroyers with no American losses. These crushing naval defeats sealed the American victory in the war. Overnight, The United States had become a dominant force in the trade relations between Europe and the Orient.

The most significant land battle in the war was the capture of San Juan Hill in Cuba on July 1st, which allowed the American forces take control of Cuba. On July 26th the Spanish Government asked the French ambassador in Washington, Jules

Cambon, to act as a liaison to discuss peace terms to end the war. The United States. and Spanish governments signed the Treaty of Paris on December 10, 1898.

The Spanish American War marked a coming-of-age for the United States as an imperial power. The treaty of Paris gave Cuba its independence from Spain and the Spanish ceded Guam and Puerto Rico to the United States. The United States agreed to pay Spain $20 million in return to gain control of the Philippines Islands.

13.2 The U.S. Senate Ratifies the Treaty of Paris on February 6, 1899.

Near the end of the war John Hay, the American ambassador to England wrote to Theodore Roosevelt, that "it has been a splendid little war; begun with the highest motives, carried on with magnificent intelligence and spirit, favored by that fortune which loves the brave,"[1] Jay's remarks reflect a new sense of imperialism that was sweeping through the United States. The defeat of Spain moved America into the top echelon of European imperialist countries. Americans now had imperial territories that stretched across the globe from Cuba and Puerto Rico to the Philippine Islands. The Spanish Empire, which once controlled all of South and Central America no longer had any direct imperial holdings in the western hemisphere. With the completion of the Panama Canal in August of 1914 the United States gained control of the traffic passing through the Ismouth of Panama.

Note

1. Cited by Freidel (1958, 3).

Chapter 14
The Russo-Japanese War

14.1 The Rivalry of Japan and Russia for Manchuria

By the end of the nineteenth century the competition for territories among European countries around the globe had reached a point where more than one country had ambitions to control the same territory. This resulted in an open invitation for countries to declare wars with the sole intention of obtaining territory.

One such rivalry was the fierce competition between Russia and Japan for control of Manchuria and Korea. By 1900 the Russians had completed construction of the trans-Siberian railroad which linked Moscow to Vladivostok, a move that greatly increased Russian presence in Manchuria. However, because the harbor at Vladivostok was closed by ice for three months of the year, the Russians still lacked a port that was open to the Pacific Ocean throughout the year. The nearest ice-free port was Port Arthur, which was located at the tip of the Liaotung Peninsula. To meet this need, the Russians built the Trans Manchurian Railway between Port Arthur and the town of Hardin, which was located on the Trans-Siberian Railway. They then built extensive fortifications around Port Arthur and stationed a portion of their Pacific Fleet there.

14.2 The Japanese Attack Russia

The Japanese, who were relative newcomers to the world of imperial expansion. regarded the Russian presence at Port Arthur as a major obstacle to their own imperial ambitions to control the Liaotung Peninsula, Manchuria, Korea part of China and were determined to check the Russian intrusion into "their part of the World." After a heated debate in the Imperial Cabinet, the Japanese government severed diplomatic relations with Russia on February 4, 1904. Four days later several destroyers of the Imperial Japanese Navy launched an attack against the Russian naval fleet moored at Port Arthur. Several Russian ships were seriously damaged by torpedoes before the Japanese ships retreated without any further action. On the same night, a group of Japanese warships attacked two Russian ships anchored at Inchon, a port on the western coast of Korea near Seoul. The next day Japan declared war against the Russian Empire, and on February 12th 3000 Japanese troops landed at Inchon and moved inland to occupy Seoul. The Japanese effort to expand their empire was under way.

At first glance the Japanese decision to start a war with the Russian Empire would seem to be a rather risky gamble. Russia had a population of 140 million; a standing army of 1.1 million men with an additional 2 million men in reserve. Japan had a population of just under 47 million men and a standing army of 283,000 men with 400,000 men in reserve. Both countries had substantial navies, though much of the Russian Navy was stationed in the Baltic Sea. The Japanese were counting on element of surprise; together with a significant advantage gained from shorter supply routes and a supreme confidence in the quality of their armed forces to produce a quick victory that would give them control of Liaotung Peninsula, Manchuria, and Korea.

14.3 The Battle of Mukden

Things did not go well for Japanese forces during the early months of the war. Attacks by Japanese troops against the forts protecting Port Arthur were repulsed with heavy casualties, and efforts by the Japanese Navy to block access to the harbor were unsuccessful. However, the Japanese persisted. By the end of December, when Port Arthur finally surrendered, the Japanese had managed to push the Russians out of the Liaotung Peninsula and into Manchuria. On February 23, 1905, the rival armies clashed near the town of Mukden. The Battle of Mukden, which lasted for two weeks, was the largest battle involving European nations since the Napoleonic Wars. Over half a million troops were engaged in the battle, and more than 35,000 men were killed in action with another 100,000 wounded. Neither side was able to gain a clear advantage and by the time the fighting finally ended, both sides were completely exhausted. The Russians retreated north to the rail junction at Harbin, while the Japanese were content to remain near Mukden to lick their wounds.

14.4 Financing the War

The Japanese were clearly winning the war on the battlefield, but even before the battle of Mukden was over, it was becoming clear that neither side could afford to sustain this fight. The Japanese forces were having a hard time supplying their troops with supplies and ammunition, and their government was finding it difficult to find a way to finance the costs of the war. In a word, the Japanese government was facing bankruptcy if they continued this level of military spending. Russia was facing an even more serious economic and political crisis that threatened to overthrow the government of Tsar Nicolas II. Both countries were looking for a graceful way out of this conflict, and on March 20th, when the President of the United States, Theodore Roosevelt, privately extended an offer to the Japanese to mediate a peace settlement, General Kodama, the Japanese chief of staff in Manchuria, hurried to Tokyo to urge the government to accept a cease fire. His concerns were supported by several ministers of the government and by the middle of April, the Japanese Cabinet was considering what they should propose in the event of a peace conference.

14.5 The Battle of Toshima

The Tsar was in less of a hurry. His generals still supported the war and consequently, sporadic skirmishes continued in Manchuria for another month. But all this changed on May 27th when the Imperial Japanese Navy under Admiral Togo Heihachro annihilated the Second Pacific Squadron of the Russian Navy in Straits of Tsushima. The Russian squadron had been hastily formed from ships in Russia's Baltic Fleet and left for Japan on October 15, 1904. They arrived in the straits between Korea and southern Japan after a seven-month odyssey of 18,000 miles and were in no condition to take on the Japanese fleet that was lying in wait for the Russian Fleet to arrive. After two days of fighting, all of the Russian battleships and all but three of their cruisers were sunk or surrendered to the enemy. Japanese losses totaled three torpedo boats.

The disaster of Tsushima, together with the growing opposition to the war throughout the Russian Empire convinced the Tsar that Russia must also find a way to end this war. On June 9th Roosevelt's offer to mediate a peace agreement between Japan and Russia was made public and both sides quickly agreed to meet in Portsmouth, New Hampshire to settle the dispute. On September 5th Russia and Japan signed the Treaty of Portsmouth ending the Russo-Japanese War. As is often the case with settlements of this sort, neither side was pleased with the terms of the treaty. The war had been a military and political disaster for the Russians. Roughly half their navy had been destroyed; control of Port Arthur and the Liaodong Peninsula were ceded to Japan; and the Imperial Japanese Navy was now the dominant force in the Pacific. The Russians were also forced to abandon their interests in Korea and Manchuria, together with the southern half of Sakhalin Island.

It is easy to conclude that Japan's gamble on a war with Russia to further their imperial ambitions was a stunning success. They had forced the Russians out of Korea and Manchuria, and they had established themselves as a major player in international politics. However, the economic costs of the war, which far exceeded anyone's expectations, brought the Japanese economy to the brink of bankruptcy. The Japanese had hoped to force the Russians to pay an indemnity to help cover the costs incurred by the war, but the Russians successfully resisted that demand. As a result, the Treaty of Portsmouth was extremely unpopular with the Japanese public,

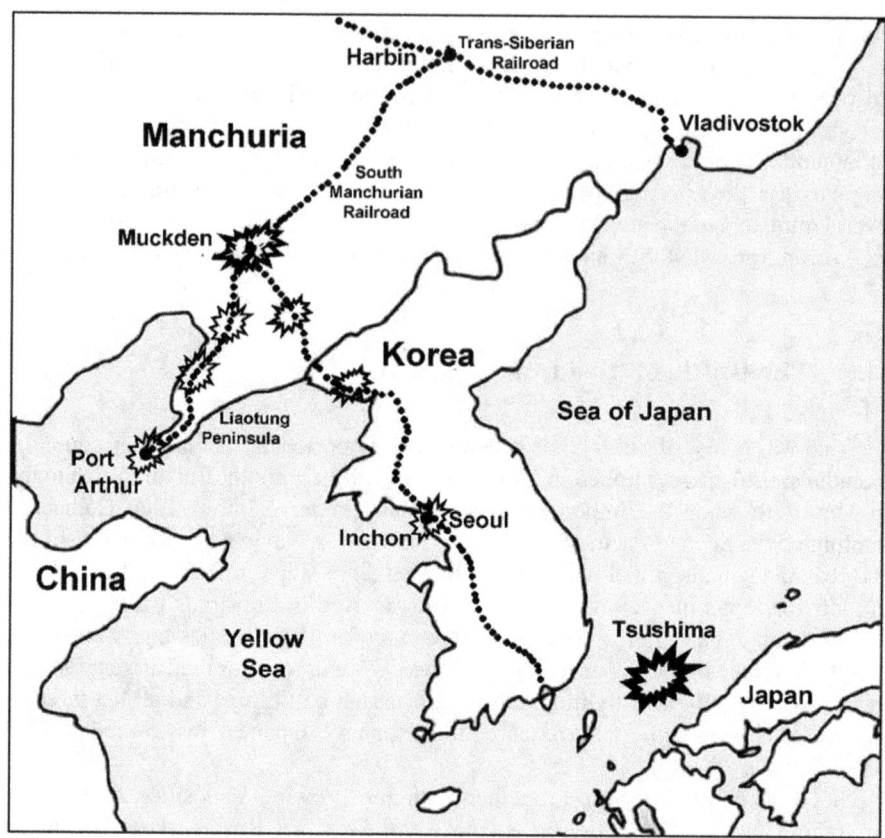

Figure 14.1 The Russo-Japanese war. *Source* Tyler (1905)

and for the time being, at least Japan's appetite for imperial expansion was satiated (Fig. 14.1).

14.6 The Emergence of Japan as an Imperial Power

Contemporaries viewed this conflict between these two imperial powers as a significant event. Sydney Tyler, a journalist who had covered a variety of conflicts including the Boer War, claimed that:

> Never since the great Napoleonic wars which convulsed Europe a century ago has the world witnessed an appeal to arms so momentous in its issues and so tremendous in its possibilities as that which has just been tried between Russia and Japan in the Far East." (Tyler 1905, p. 8)

14.6 The Emergence of Japan as an Imperial Power

Table 14.1 Japanese military and economic advancement—1890–1910

Year	MILEX	MILPER	IRST	PEC	TOTPOP	UPOP	%CINC
1890	3905.0	71.0	19.0	2830	39,902	2469	2.14
1895	**11,743.0**	**207.0**	**24.0**	**5074**	**41,557**	**2637**	**3.12**
1900	13,311.0	182.0	1.0	8010	43,847	3856	2.89
1905	**73,031.0**	**250.0**	**71.0**	**12,397**	**46,620**	**4833**	**4.85**
1910	18,516.0	283.0	168.0	16,678	49,184	5898	3.50

Tyler's hyperbolic prose seems a bit exaggerated when viewed through the shadow cast by the "Great War" that broke out in Europe only a few years later. But he had a point. By 1910 Japan had emerged as an Imperial Power in the Orient.

Table 14.1 illustrates the speed with which Japan became an important player in the world of imperial states. Specifically, there are large jumps in 1895 and 1905, both times when Japan went to war. In 1890 the Japanese were still a small country off the coast of China that was just getting imperial ambitions. By 1910 they were able to challenge to the point where they were able to challenge the Russians for control of Eastern Manchuria.

Chapter 15
The Schlieffen Plan

15.1 World Empires in 1900

By the end of the nineteenth century the European imperial powers had exhausted the list of territories that might expand their empires without offending some other country. Figure 15.1 shows a map of the imperial empires of the world in 1900. The British Empire was by far the largest Empire among the European states, stretching from Canada to Australia and including India and a major part of East Africa. The French Empire was the second largest, with substantial holdings in North Africa and Southeast Asia. The Portuguese, Italians, Dutch, Germans, and Belgians all had smaller Imperial holdings in Africa and the Pacific islands. The Russians and Chinese controlled large areas of Asia simply because of the size of their countries. What was left of the Ottoman Empire controlled a major part of the Middle East.

15.2 The Schlieffen Plan

All of the larger states of Europe jealously protected the territories they governed, and most of them sought some sort of added protection by forming alliances with other imperial states to come to their aid if they were attacked. The result of all this was to create a situation where any military action by a state against another state was likely to touch off attacks from other states willing to help their ally. In a remark that he made in 1888, Otto von Bismark remarked that "One day the great European war will come out of some damned foolish thing in the Balkans."

In November 1891 Kaiser Wilhelm II appointed Alfred von Schlieffen as the commander of the German Army; a position he would hold until 1906. Schlieffen's first challenge was to deal with threat posed by the alliance that France and Russia had made in 1894 to come to each other's aid in the event of an attack from another power Schlieffen and his colleagues firmly believed that France had not yet recovered

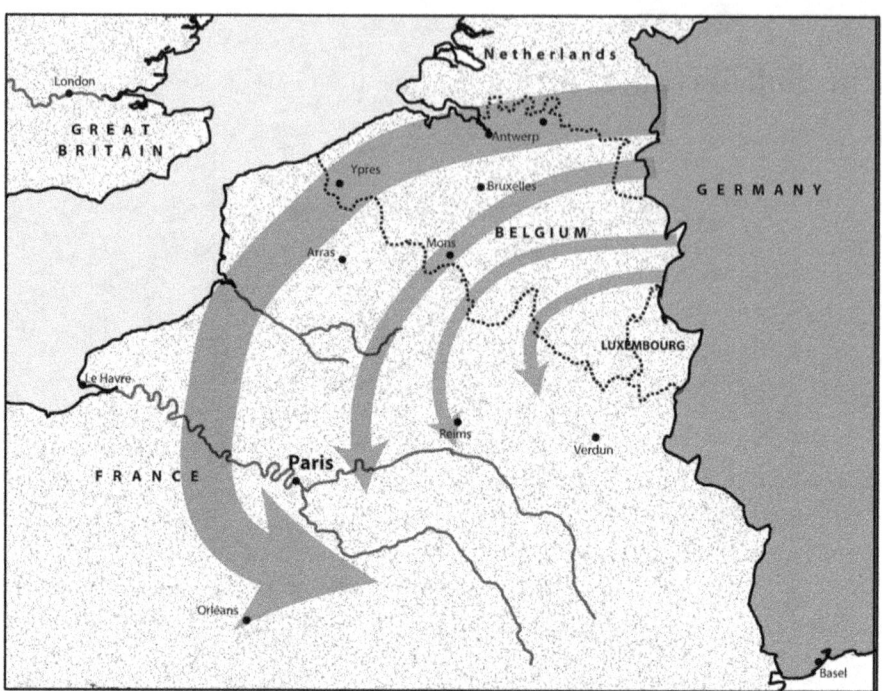

Fig. 15.1 The Schlieffen plan. *Sources* Ransom (2018), Hanson (2001) and Clodfelter (2015)

from their disastrous defeat in the Franco-Prussian war, and they were confident that the French would eventually seek another war with Germany. The Franco-Russian alliance of 1894 created a situation where such a war with either France or Russia would mean Germany would have to face a two-front war with both France and Russia.

Schlieffen's solution to a situation where Germany faced a war with either France or Russia was for Germany to immediately invade France. His reasoning was that the Germans could defeat France—as they had in the Franco-Prussian War—and then they could deal with Russia. By the time he retired in 1906 he had outlined a plan for the invasion of France. The core of his approach was that two thirds of the German army was placed ahead on the right flank of the German Army. These troops would sweep through the Netherlands and Belgium in a wide arc along the east coast of the English Channel until they were southeast of Paris. They would then be in a position to attack Paris from the south and repeat the victory of the Franco-Prussian war. Figure 15.2 shows how the plan should work.

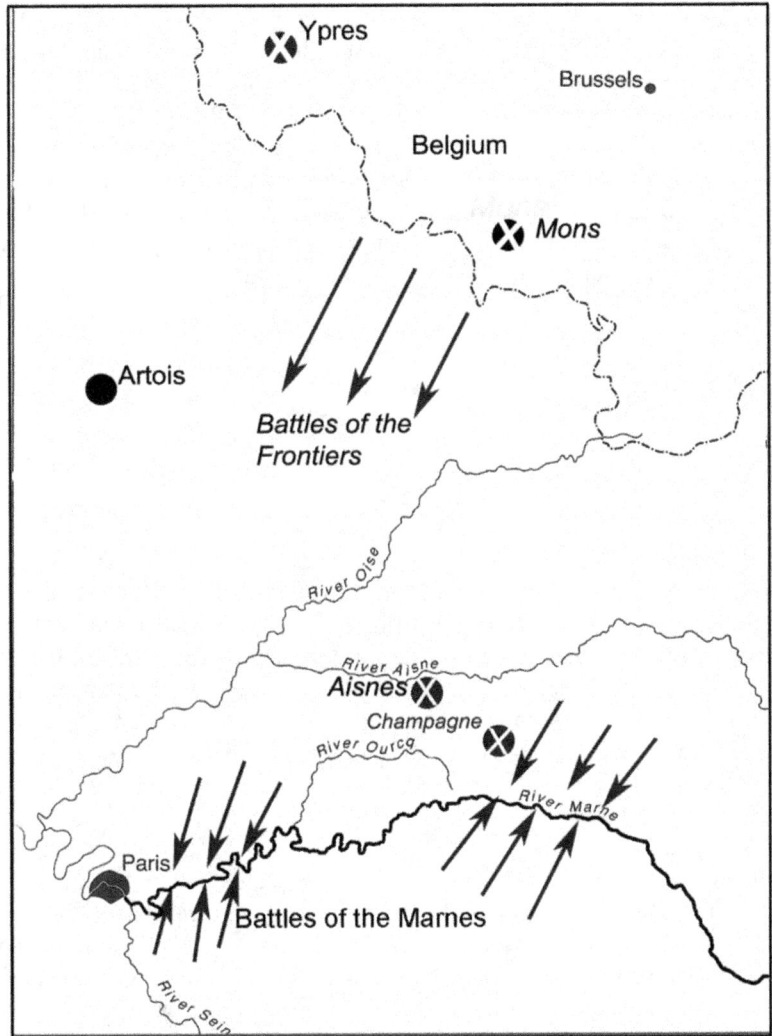

Fig. 15.2 Early battles on the western front. *Sources* Ransom (2018) and Clodfelter (2015)

15.3 The Assassination of the Archduke Ferdinand

In July of 1914 Archduke Franz Ferdinand was killed by a group known as the *Black Hand*. When Austria insisted that the Serbian Government take action against the group, the Serbian government refused. After confirming the support of their German allies and effectively receiving a "Blank Check" to do what they felt was necessary to curb the Black Hand, the Habsburg Empire invaded Serbia on July 28th.

Schlieffen did not say *why* Russia might go to war with Germany in 1914. He was focused on possibility that the 1894 alliance of France and Russia could start a war between the two countries. He certainly did not anticipate how the Archduke's assassination would lead to a war between Germany and Russia.

There were two sets of alliances that governed who should help their allies in the event of a military conflict. The *Triple Entente Powers* consisting of Russia, France, and the British Empire, and the *Triple Alliance* consisting of The Hapsburg Empire, Germany, and Italy—though Italy initially made it clear that they wanted to stay out of any conflicts that came from the Archdukes assignation.

15.4   The Invasion of France in 1914

Unfortunately for the Germans, plans don't always work out the way they are supposed to. By 1914 the head of the German Army was Helmuth von Moltke—a nephew of the Helmuth von Moltke who commanded the German armies during the Franco-Prussian war. Moltke was not happy that Schlieffen's plan had the German army invading both Belgium and the Netherlands. "I cannot agree" he wrote in a memo written in 1911, "that Dutch neutrality needs to be violated. The Netherlands at our rear could have disastrous consequences for the advance of the German Army to the West." To avoid violating Dutch territory, Moltke moved the planned invasion route far enough to the east to avoid the Netherland's borders, a change that made the German attack on Paris more difficult. The arrival of French forces at the Battles of the Frontiers and the appearance of the British Expeditionary Forces [BEF] at the Battle of Mons at the beginning of August 1914 forced the German invaders to move even further to the east.

By the end of August, the German columns had ground to a halt. Schlieffen had been adamant that the right flank of the German Army must reach all the way to the English Channel and historians have been quick to blame Von Moltke for making adjustments to the invasion route that prevented the Germans from capturing Paris—which had been a critical part off Schlieffen's plan. However, the change in the German invasion route was not the only thing that foiled the Germans. The Entente Commanders had elected to attack the advancing German invaders in a series of encounters known as the "First Battle of the Marne." Entente Forces were able to push the Germans into a retreat north to the River Marne, and at this point the German defenses stiffened, and they were able to prevent the French from pushing them any further north.

Simply put, this meant that a pivotal part of the Schlieffen Plan was missing. The Germans were able to remain in Northern France for the remainder of the war, but the French had successfully defended Paris and forced the German invasion stop at the River Marne.

15.5 The Race to the Sea

Both sides now began what became what historians have called "The Race to the Sea," which was a series of battles that lasted the rest of summer and into the late fall of 1914 as the armies moved North slowly towards the English Channel. Neither side "won" the Race. Figure 15.2 shows a map of the "Western Front" in September 1914. What eventually emerged from the early battles of the war was long lists of casualties on both sides of the war and a line of trenches that eventually stretched from Ypres, Belgium to the Swiss Border. A year of fighting in 1914 produced 1.1 million casualties for the French, British, and German armies fighting on the Western Front in 1914 (Table 15.1).

15.6 Stalemate on the Western Front

A year of fighting in 1914 had produced more than a million casualties for the French, British, and German armies fighting on the Western Front in 1914. Neither side had gained any advantage from the stalemate that had emerged on the Western Front by the end of 1914.

All through the summer of 1915 the French and the British armies pounded the German defenses, and when a charge failed, they usually went back and tried again. Sites in the trenches such as Ypres, Artois, and Champagne all experienced several major attacks by Allied forces, but the German lines did not yield any significant territory. During the course of the year the total area recovered by the Entente Forces from these attacks in 1914 was only 8 square miles of the 19,500 square miles of France and Belgium occupied by the Germans as of the first day of 1915 (Clodfelter, 2015, 395).

What is truly astounding about these statistics is the willingness of generals at all levels of rank in both armies to accept the enormous casualties suffered in these attacks. And the worst was still to come. The two largest battles of this war were the German attacks on the city of Verdun, which started on February 21, 1916, and lasted for 303 days and produced at least 700,00 French and German casualties. Some estimates place the total cost of the two battles at over 800,000 dead or wounded. The other battle with horrific casualties was the British attack on German lines along the area near the Somme River, which began on July 1st. In this battle—which was intended to draw German troops away from the battle for Verdun—the British suffered 57,479 casualties on the first day of battle. The British and Germans together suffered over a million casualties before the battle on the Somme ended on November 18th. Estimates of the total number of casualties for the entire Western Front in 1916 were a staggering two and a half million men, with little to show for their efforts.

Both sides were looking for a way to break the stalemate on the Western Front.

Table 15.1 The race to the sea

Battles	Total forces	Casualties	Percent casualties	Date
Frontiers				August 24–25
French	1,250,000	260,000	20.80	
German	750,000	220,000	29.33	
Mons				25-August
British	72,000	4244	5.89	
German	135,000	5000	3.70	
First Marne				September 5–11
Germans	900,000	4244	0.47	
Allies	1,080,000	5000	0.46	
First Aisne				September 13–27
Allies	1,080,000	150,000		
German	900,000			
First Ypres				October 20–November 24
British	407,085	50,000	12.28	
French	100,000	50,000	50.00	
German	134,315	31,265	23.28	
Total losses for 1914				
French				
British				
German				

Chapter 16
The Sideshows: Italy, Gallipoli, and the Middle East

16.1 The Russian Invasion of East Prussia

The Western front of the First World War has received most of the attention from historians of the First World War because of the size of the battles that were raging and the fact that it was likely that whoever won these battles was likely to win this war. However, the Western Front was not the only place where the Entente Allies and Central Powers confronted each other. In 1915. Schlieffen had been confident that the Germans would be able to handle any attempt by the Russians to interfere with their war with France. His confidence was well-placed. In August of 1914 a Russian Army of more than a million Russian troops threatened the border of east Prussia.

The Russians faced a German army that was led by Paul von Hindenburg—who had been called out of retirement so hastily that he did not have time get an up-to-date uniform. With Eric Ludendorff as his partner, the Hindenburg-Ludendorff team formed one of the best commanders in the entire war. They managed to out-maneuver a Russian army at the battle of Tannenberg and inflicted a defeat so serious that the Russian General, Alexander Samsonov, committed suicide after the battle. They followed their success at Tannenberg by winning two additional victories over the disorganized Russian Army at Masurium Lakes.

By the end of 1915 the Central Powers were ready to invade Russia and feed their imperial appetite by gaining some territory along their Western border, and the Entente Powers were still desperately looking for some way to break the stalemate on the Western Front and strengthen their position in the Eastern theater of the War (Fig. 16.1).

At this point Winston Churchill, the First Lord of the British Admiralty, came up with a novel idea. He suggested that the Allies should launch an offensive to gain control of the Dardanelles; an action that would draw troops away from the stalemate of the Western Front, isolate the Ottoman capital of Constantinople, and separate the European and Asian parts of the Ottoman Empire from each other. Churchill got the French to support the idea, and the British and the French navies assembled a fleet

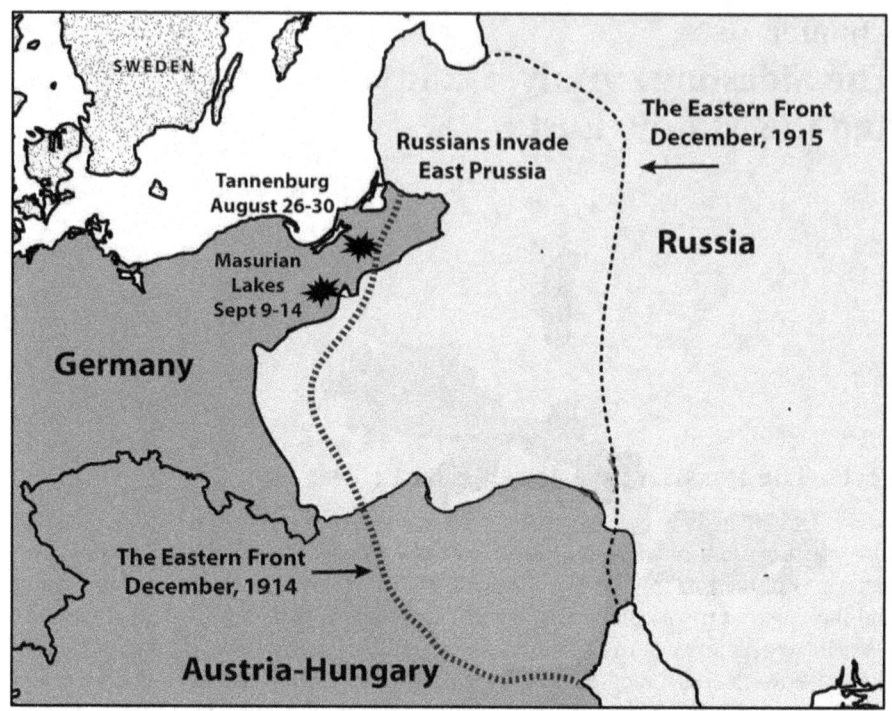

Fig. 16.1 The eastern front in 1915–16. *Sources* Ransom (2018) and Clodfelter (2015)

of 90 warships to attack the water connection between the Black Sea and the Aegean Sea and on to the Mediterranean Sea (see Fig. 16.2).

Efforts by the Entente navies to clear the channel from the Black Sea to the Sea of Marmara through the Bosphorus Straits were not successful, so the Allies decided to land troops on Gallipoli; a peninsula that guards the southern route between Istanbul and the Aegean Sea.

The naval attack went well enough. On April 25, 1915 the large guns of the Allied battle ships managed to silence the Ottoman guns without losing any ships—though three ships were damaged by mines. However, when the ANZAC troops from Australia and New Zealand tried to make landings on the northwestern coast of Gallipoli, the Turkish infantry protecting the heights overlooking the waterway forced them to retreat back to the beaches after suffering heavy losses. For the next three months the Turks continued to repel a flurry of ANZAC infantry attacks, and the battle for control of the Gallipoli Peninsula became a stalemate to match the struggle on the Western Front. By the end of 1915, the Allies were willing to give up and go home. In what was one of the few successful maneuvers of the Gallipoli Campaign, almost all of the allied troops were safely evacuated from the peninsula during the last week of December 1915 and the first two weeks of January 1916.

16.2 Italy Changes Sides

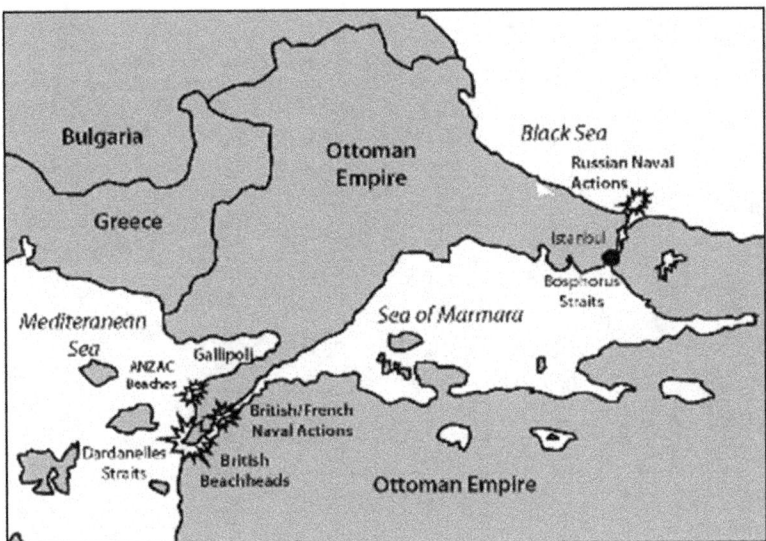

Fig. 16.2 The Gallipoli campaign. *Source* Ransom (2018)

The Gallipoli Campaign turned out to be an unmitigated disaster for the Allied forces. Out of 410,000 British Empire soldiers who fought on the peninsula, 31,389 were killed or missing and 78,749 were wounded. Of the 500,000 Turks who fought in the same battles, 250,000 became casualties (Clodfelter 2015, 418). The Turks could claim that they had managed to retain their control of the Gallipoli Peninsula and the route between the Mediterranean Sea and Istanbul; while the Allies were left still searching for some way to break the stalemate on the Western Front.

Though the Gallipoli campaign was a failure, it did signal an expansion of interest on the part of the Allied forces in their battle with the Ottoman Empire. The entry of the Turks into the war on the side of the Central Powers had made the Middle East an important part of the struggle (Table 16.1).

16.2 Italy Changes Sides

The decision by the Ottoman Empire to enter the war as a partner of the Central Powers was not the only change in the alignment of major powers fighting the war in 1915. At the outset of the fighting in April of 1914 Italy had announced that they would remain neutral in the war. However, Italy had been struggling with Austria-Hungary over territory surrounding their northern border with Austria-Hungary. On April 26, 1915, the Italians secretly signed an agreement to join the Entente Powers. In exchange for their commitment to fight with the Allies, the Italians were promised

16 The Sideshows: Italy, Gallipoli, and the Middle East

Table 16.1 The eastern front: 1914–1918

Battle	Total forces	Casualties	Percent casualties	Date
Tannenburg				August 6–31
Russia	250,000	30,000	12.00	
German		3000	6.50	
First Masuriaan lakes				
Russian	200,000	5000	37.50	September 5–13
German	250,000	10,000	4.00	
Galicia				
Russian	750,000	210,000	28.00	
Austrian	500,000	30.000	2.00	
Second Masurian Lake				February 7–21
5. Russian		56,000		
9. German		75,000		
Gorlice Tarnow				May 2–June 27
Russian		200,00		
German		126,000		
Austria		87,000		
Brusilov offensives				June 4–September 20
Russa		130,000		
German		150,000		
Austria		614,000		

that the Allies would support their claim to the contested territory if the Allies won the war.

On April 26, 1915 the Italians, who had announced that they were neutral at the outbreak of the war, secretly signed the Treaty of London and joined the Entente Allies, the Treaty of London promised them the land they wanted from the Austrians, so the Italians chose to join Britain and France in the war against the Central Powers.

Italy's decision to join the war in 1915 produced a fierce struggle with Austria-Hungary. Over the course of the next three years, the Italians and the Austrians fought eleven battles in the Izono Mountains of Northern Italy with neither side emerging as a clear winner. That changed in May of 1917 when the Germans agreed to send seven divisions commanded by General Otto von Below to support an Austrian request for German help in breaking through their Italian Front. Von Bellow's men were veterans of the battle at Verdun, and on October 24th they managed to create a huge hole in the Italian lines along the north bank of the Piave River. The Italian army simply disintegrated. They suffered 12,000 men killed and 23,000 wounded and the Germans took 275,000 prisoners. It is likely that an equal number ot men simply deserted (Clodfelter 2015, 420). Fortunately for the Italians, a torrential rain

16.2 Italy Changes Sides

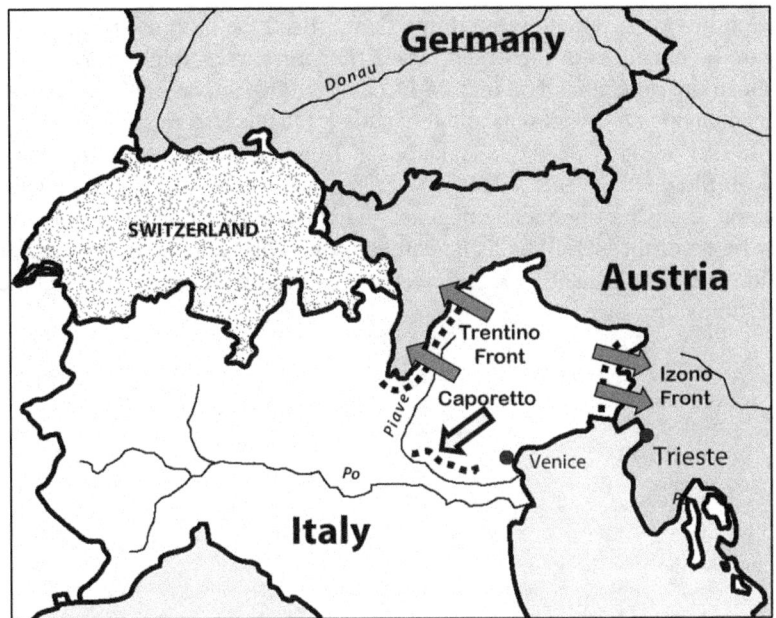

Fig. 16.3 The Italian front. Sources Ransom (2018) and Clodfelter (2015)

storm made the Piave River difficult to cross, and the Austrian and German troops were forced to stop at north bank of the river (Fig. 16.3).

The Allied command feared that the disaster of Caporetto was serious enough that it might cause Italy to drop out of the war. They rushed four French and two British divisions to Italy to help shore up the Italian defenses along the North Bank of Piave River. The arrival of these fresh troops helped the Italians stop the further advance of the Austrian troops, and at this point Ludendorff—who had never been in favor of sending a large number of troops to the Italian Front—pulled back most of the German support for the Austrians. On October 24, 1918,—exactly a year after the Caporetto disaster—the Italians decisively defeated the Austrians in the battle of Vittorio-Veneto. Immediately after this battle the Austrians asked for an armistice that effectively ended the War between Italy and the Ottoman Empire.

Egypt and Palestine were now open to possible attacks from the Ottoman Empire forces. Most of the Entente troops that were taken off the Gallipoli Peninsula were therefore transferred to Egypt, and by the end of 1916 more than 400,000 British troops had been reorganized to form the Egyptian Expeditionary Force [EEF] under the command of Sir Archibald Murray.

Murray's task was to capture Jerusalem and move north to Damascus and Istanbul. Things did not start well for the British. Several efforts to force the Turks out of Gaza were unsuccessful, and in October of 1917 Murray was replaced by Edmund Allenby, a general who had been successful with mounted troops in the African Boer Wars. Allenby abandoned the trench warfare employed on the Western Front and replaced it with a more open approach to fighting that utilized the mobility of the Entente's cavalry in the openness of the desert. The EEF forces were able to force the Turks out of Gaza on November 6th, and on December 9th they entered Jerusalem. The path was then open to Damascus and to Istanbul. On the eastern side of the Arabian Peninsula EEF troops forced the Turks out of Kut-el-Amara and managed to reach Bagdad on March 11, 1917. Allenby's strategy was to conduct a mobile war with cavalry and keep the opponent off guard, which proved to be highly successful. The key battle of the Sinai Peninsula campaign was on September 19–21, 1918, at Megiddo, where the Entente forces defeated the Ottoman forces and ended the war for the Ottoman Empire.

Chapter 17
Palestine and Sykes-Picot

17.1 The Sykes-Picot Agreement

Well before the Battle of Megiddo, British and the French military leaders were confident that the Ottoman Empire would be defeated. The question then would be: How should the territory that was formerly claimed by the Ottoman Empire be divided into political entities after the fighting ended? To answer that question the British and French Governments formed a committee in November of 1915 to outline how the territories of the Ottoman Empire should be governed after the war. The Sykes-Picot Agreement takes its name from the two representatives—both of whom had worked on drafting the map that would delineate a new political arrangement for what had once been the Ottoman Empire.

Sykes for Britain and Georges Picot for France; drafted a new map for what had once been the Ottoman Empire. Sykes was a colonel in the British army who was familiar with the Ottoman Empire and knew most of the prominent British politicians who were working on the committee charged with the task of redefining the boundaries of the Ottoman Empire. Georges Picot was a veteran French diplomat who also had experience working with the politics of the Middle East. Through December of 1915 these two men secretly met at the French Embassy in London on a daily basis to hammer out the details of which countries would have control of various parts of the Arabian Peninsula. They presented their map to the committee on May 16, 1916, and it was secretly endorsed by both Britain and France. Figure 17.1 presents a map of the Sykes-Picot proposal as it was reported to the Committee.

The map that Sykes and Picot presented to the committee in May of 1916 was careful to take note of what the various major powers wanted. The British were primarily concerned that they retain control or influence on an area that would protect their interests in Egypt, the Suez Canal, and territory along the Western coast of the Persian Gulf. The French were primarily concerned with an area in the north of the Arabian Peninsula. The Russians were mainly concerned that they protect an area of

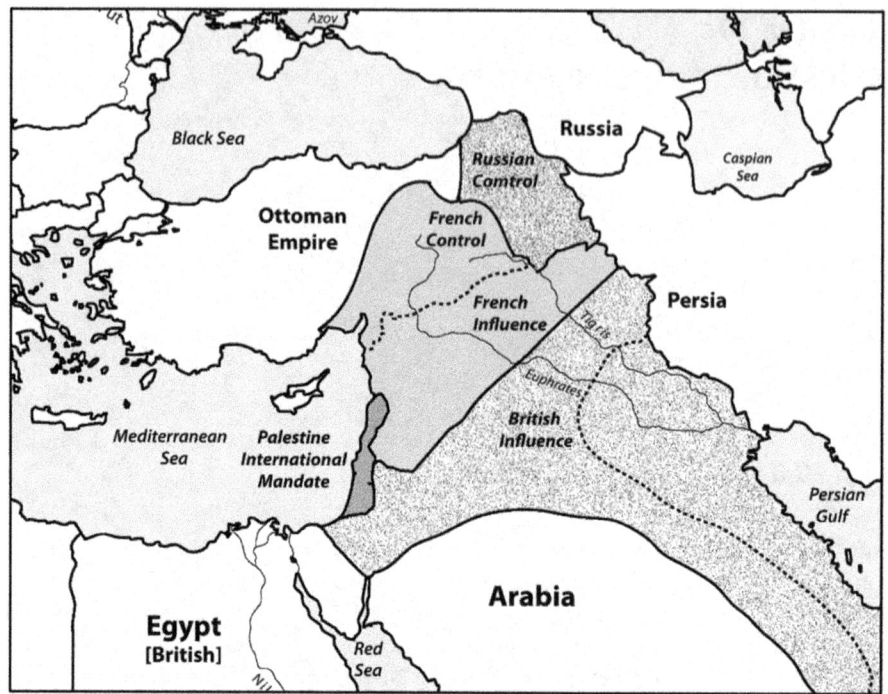

Fig. 17.1 The Sykes-picot map. *Source* Ransom (2018)

the Arabian Peninsula that touched upon the southern border of Russia. The Sykes-Picot map that was secretly presented to the Committee map met all these broad interests. They were not made public until 1918 when Vladimir Lenin released them after the Soviet Government signed the Treaty of Brest-Litovsk had been signed by the Soviet Government in 1918.

Chapter 18
The Treaty of Brest-Litovsk

18.1 Brest-Litovsk

By the Spring of 1918 the success of the German military effort on the Eastern Front, together with the political turmoil associated with the abdication of Czar Nicholas, which involved the formation of a new Soviet Government headed by Vladimir Lenin, to seek a peaceful end to the war with the Central Powers. On March 3, 1918, Lenin signed the Treaty of Brest-Litovsk with Germany, Austria-Hungary, the Ottoman Empire, and Bulgaria, ending the Soviet Government's participation in the imperial war with the Central Powers.

The immediate effect of the Treaty was that it allowed the Germans to move troops that had been fighting on the Eastern Front to reinforce the troops fighting on the Western Front. The other, and equally important change, was that the Russians put a clause in the treaty that ceded a huge amount of territory that was currently occupied by German troops—most of Finland, the Baltic provinces, parts of Poland, and parts of the Ukraine would now be part of the German Empire (See Fig. 18.1). With the stroke of a few pens, the signatures on treaty of Brest-Litovsk turned Germany into a major imperial power in the center of Europe, and the Germans were more willing to use their newfound military power to fight any threat on the part of a European power who might challenge their claim to the conquered territory.

No one could be happier with this situation than Adolf Hitler. While he was still in prison at Landsberg Hitler had written a second manuscript that was apparently intended to be a sequel to *Mein Kampf*. The existence of this manuscript, which was not found until 1958, and was not published until 1961, presented a clear blueprint for the policies which he would implement if he were ever to gain power. At the center of those plans was the need to expand Germany's boundaries to include populations that Hitler regarded as "German." The borders of Bismarck's Reich, according to Hitler, "encompassed only a part of the German nation." The pre-1914 borders, he claimed, "ran straight across German language areas, and even through parts which, at least formerly, had belonged to the German Union, even if in an informal way"

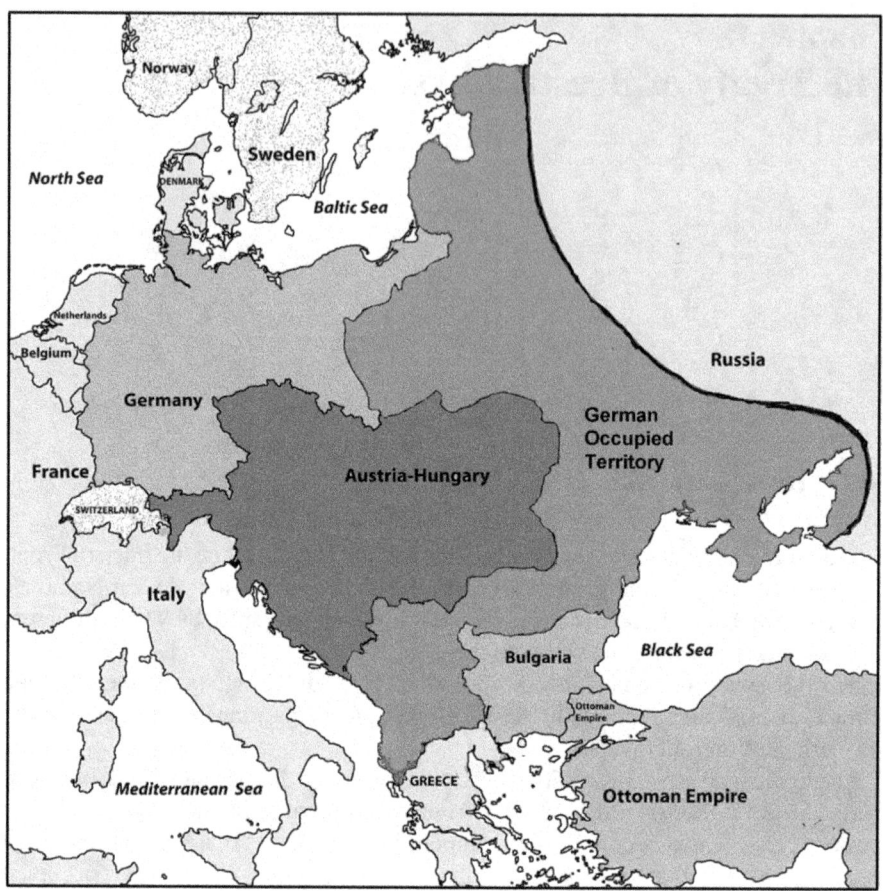

Fig. 18.1 German occupied territory. *Source* Ransom (2018)

(Hitler 1961, 48–9). Hitler made it clear that he intended to see that the German state reclaimed these areas. "No foreign policy aim," he wrote, "could have been more obvious for the strictly formal national state of that time than the annexation of those German areas in Europe which, partly through their former history, had to be an obvious part not only of the German nation but of a German Reich" (Hitler 1961, 56). Russia's departure from the war between Central Powers and Entente Powers turned that conflict into an Imperial War. And at least for the time being, Germany was holding a favorable hand for the imperialists (See Fig. 18.1).

18.2 The United States Enters the War

A third development that affected Ludendorff's planning for 1918 was that the United States had finally decided to join the war on the side of the Entente Powers. President Woodrow Wilson had asked Congress for "a war to end all wars" that would "make the world safe for democracy," and Congress had agreed. By the end of March 1918, about 300,000 American troops were on their way to Europe, and Entente Powers were expected to have over a million troops by the end of the year (Clodfelter 2015, 402). Ludendorff and Hindenburg could see that the Germans had two options. They could sit on their gains and hope to negotiate a peace with the Entente Powers; or they could take advantage of Russia's withdrawal from the war to make one more effort to finally break the stalemate on the Western front.

Chapter 19
The Ludendorff Offensives

19.1 Imperialism and Ludendorff's Imperial War

General Eric Ludendorff was an eager imperialist. He argued that if the Germans could quickly move about 750,000 German Troops from the Eastern and Italian Fronts to fight on the Western Front, the Germans could quickly add even more imperial gains to their Empire. The allies had no obvious response to such a large movement in German troops; the only question was whether or not there was enough time for the Germans to make use of this advantage to break through the Entente lines. Ludendorff was convinced that there was enough time, and he convinced Hindenburg and the Kaiser that they should begin an accelerated program of training German troops for a major offensive in the spring of 1918.

When the spring of 1918 arrived, the Gartman troops were in place and what would become known as *Kaiserschlacht* ("The Kaiser's Battle") or the "Ludendorff Offensives" were ready to go. The German plan was to hit the Entente forces with a massive attack by German troops who had been specially prepared to create gaps in the British and French armies before the Americans could arrive. Figure 20.2 shows where these attacks took place in the summer of 1918.

19.2 Operation Michael

The first and largest of the German attacks, code named "Operation Michael," was aimed at the point where the British and French forces met each other about 40 miles south of Arras (See Fig. 17.2). If successful, German forces would push the British forces north towards the English Channel, and push the French forces south to protect Paris. This would produce a large gap in the Entente line which would enable the rest of the German forces to surge through gap the towards Paris.

Operation Michael. which was launched on March 21, 1918, caught the British by surprise, and it pushed the British lines back for about 60 miles.

19.3 "Operation Georgette"

But the Entente infantry lines did not break. After a month of furious fighting, the Germans decided to reinforce Michael, and they launched a second attack, code named "Georgette," which was at the northern end of the British lines around Ypres (See Fig. 19.2). However, the British infantry lines once again held firm.

19.4 "Operation Blucher-Yorck"

At this point, the Germans decided to reinforce Operation Michael by launching a third attack on May 27th, with the codename of "Blucher-Yorck." This was an attack on the center of the British lines, and it got close enough to Paris that the French capital was in range of the long-range German artillery units surrounding the city. But the German infantry still could not establish a break in the lines of the Entente infantry. A follow-up action that was added to the Blucher-Yorck attack, code named "Gneisenau" was quickly launched on June 9th in a final but still unsuccessful, effort to create a gap between the British and French forces.

19.5 Ludendorff's Results

All of Ludendorff's attacks had failed to break the Entente Lines. The German Generals were forced to concede that they could not gain a victory in the war before the Americans arrived.

In the spring of 1918, the German generals were willing to accept Ludendorff's gamble that they could force the Entente into a situation of accepting an end to the war where the Germans would have almost doubled the size of their Empire and made Germany the strongest military state in Europe. The basic assumption behind Ludendorff's Offensives was that, with Russia out of the war, the Germans could move enough troops quickly enough from the eastern front to the Western Front to create a break in the Entente lines. Table 19.1 shows that in fact, there was indeed a dramatic increase in both the number of troops and the level of the military expenditures favoring the Central Powers in late 1917. But, as events turned out, this was not enough to create a collapse in the Entente Line (Fig. 19.1).

19.6 The Allies Fight Back

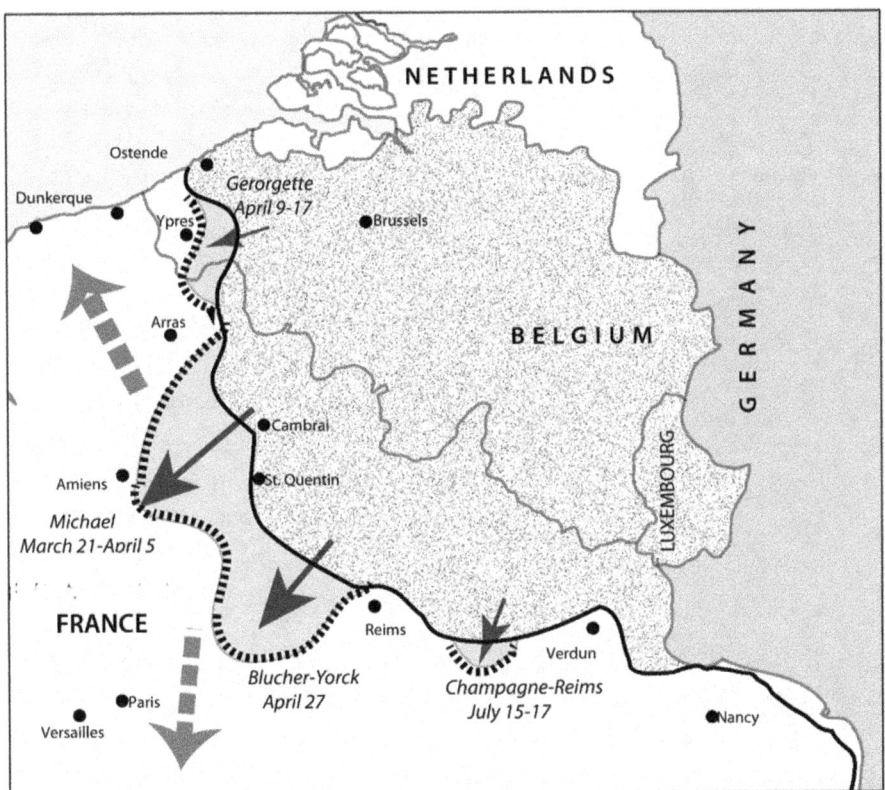

Fig. 19.1 The Ludendorff offensives. *Source* Ransom (2018) and Clodfelter (2015)

19.6 The Allies Fight Back

The steady arrival of the American troops gave General Ferdinand Foche, the Entente's new Commander in Chief, a chance to reorganize his forces into four armies. Figure 19.2 shows the deployment of forces on the Western Front in the spring of 1918. An Army of 190,000 Belgians commanded by King Albert would attack the Ypres Battlefield one more time. A British force of 1.8 million men under Sir Douglas Haig would attack the German defenders east of Aras. A French force of 2.6 million men commanded by Phillipe Petain would attack the lines at Reims, and American army of 1.9 million men under John Pershing that would attack the southern end of the line. Facing these forces was an exhausted German Army totaling 3.6 million men.

Foche's strategy was simple: Attack!!! So, the Entente Forces attacked. Table 19.1 presents data on the size and casualties from battles on the Western Front in 1918. These were big battles that the Germans could ill-afford to lose at this point of the war. However, it was clear to Ludendorff and Hindenburg by the end of September,

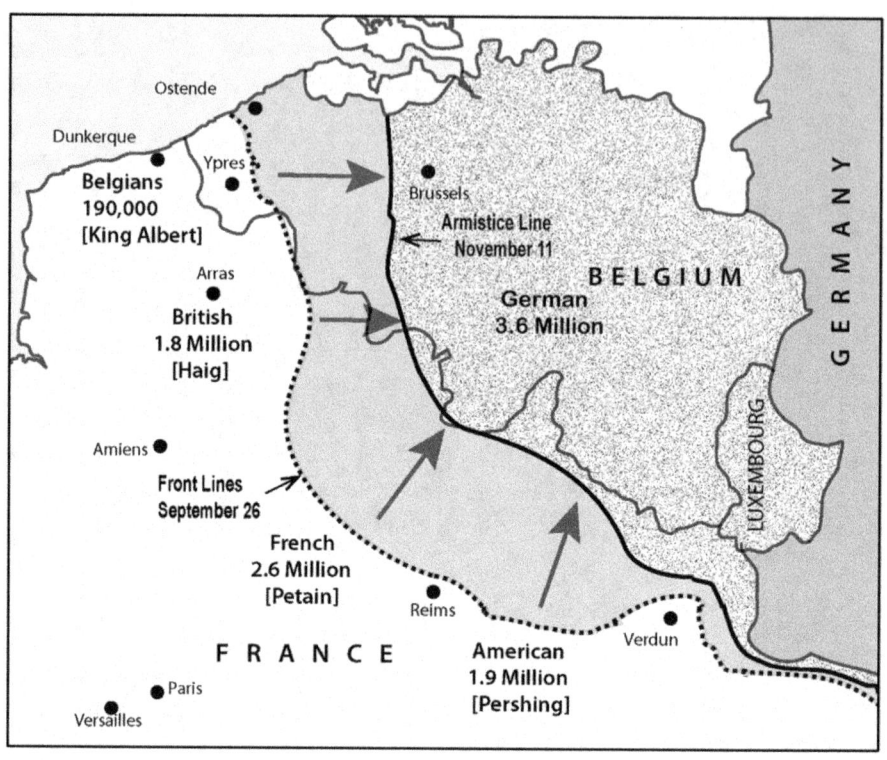

Fig. 19.2 The last offensive. *Sources* Ransom (2018) and Clodfelter (2015)

that the German Army was not going to prevent the Entente Powers from invading Germany. Moreover, it was clear that the Western Front was not the only place where the Central Powers were losing the war. German armies were reeling from Entente offensives in Greece, where the Entente Forces were pushing back the Ottoman forces. They were facing defeat in Italy, where the Ottoman forces had caved.

19.7 The Generals Throw in the Towel

On September 29th Hindenburg and Ludendorff met with the Kaiser and told him that he must resign, and Germany must request an immediate cease fire from the Entente. They pointed out that the Western front was not the only place where the Central Powers were collapsing. Figure 19.3 points out all of the various fronts where Germany and her partners were facing imminent defeat in Italy, Greece, and where the Ottoman Empire had called for a cease fire after battle of Vittorio-Veneto.

The Kaiser stubbornly resisted demands to resign as long as there was at least a faint hope that the Ludendorff Offensives might succeed. However, by November

19.7 The Generals Throw in the Towel

Table 19.1 The Ludendorff offensives

Battles	Nationality	Casualties	Date
Second Somme [Michael]			Mar 21–April 8
	French	77,000	
	British	160,000	
	German	239,00	
19 Lys [Georgette]			April 9–29
	French	35,000	
	British	76,300	
	Portuguese	7300	
	German	109,300	
128			
Third Aisne [Bucker-Yorck]			May 27–June 6
	French	98,160	
	British	25,703	
	German	56,000	
Belleau Woods [Gneisenau]			June 6–July 1
	Americans	9777	
	French	39,466	
	German	30,000	
Noyon-Montdidier' [Gneisenau]			June 9–16
French		39,466	
German		30,000	
Champagne-Marne			July 15–17
[Amiens]	Entente Forces	45,000	
	German	50,000	
Aisne-Marne			July 18–August 5
	French	98,160	
	British	28,703	
	American	5000	
	German	50,000	
Amiens			August 8–September 4
The 100 Day offensive	British	22,202	
	French	24,232	
	German	45,000	
	American	7,000	
St. Mihael			September 12–16
	Americans	127,063	
	French	50,000	

(continued)

Table 19.1 (continued)

Battles	Nationality	Casualties	Date
	German	100,000	
Meuse-Argonne			September 26–November 11
100 Day Offensive	Americans	120,063	
	French	50,000	
	German	100,000	
Total Losses 1918			
	French	511,484	
	British	237,908	
	American	268,903	
	Portuegese	7,300	
	German	468,300	

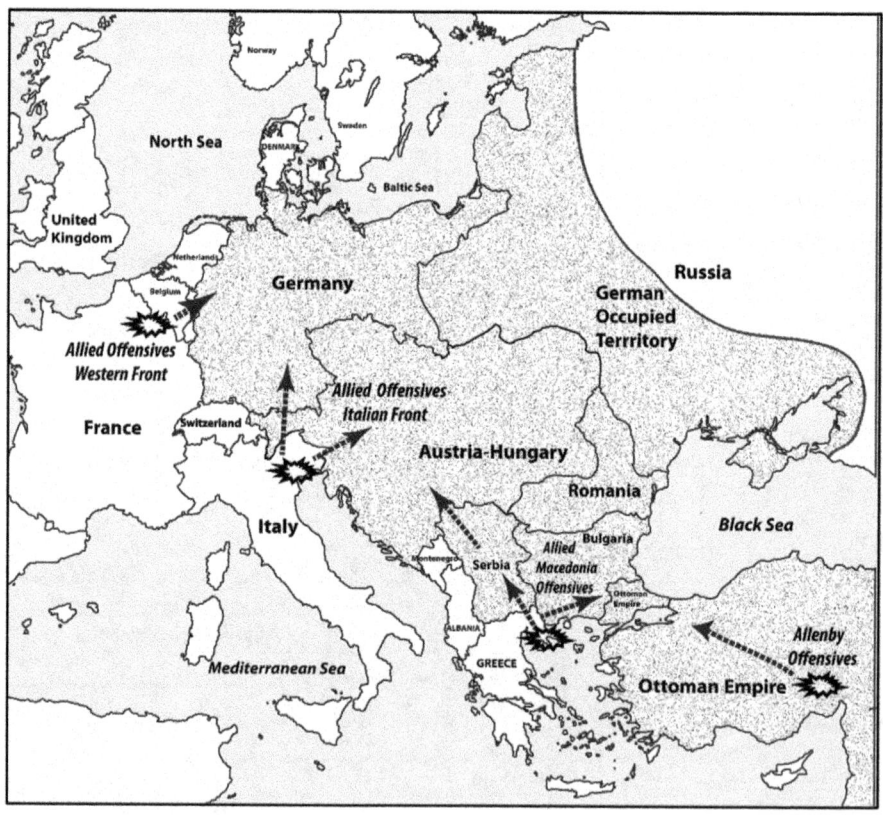

Fig. 19.3 Collapse of the central powers. *Source* Ransom (2018)

9th the generals were finally able to convince him to abdicate his throne and leave for Holland so that a civilian German government could negotiate an armistice with the Entente Leaders. Two days later the two sides finally agreed to an armistice that ended the fighting.

No one likes to lose a war. They become particularly upset if they believe their troops were winning the war when it abruptly ended. In November of 1918 a significant portion of the German population was convinced that their armies were winning the war, and they looked for scapegoats to explain why the German high command agreed to a cease fire. Adolf Hitler was particularly outraged about the terms of the cease fire, labeling the pacifists "November Criminals" who were.

Giving away the hard-earned gains of four years of armed struggle.

19.8 The Collapse of the Central Powers

In fact, the Germans were doing nothing of the sort. Not only were the Entente forces threatening to break through the Western Front; Fig. 19.3 shows that things were going just as bad elsewhere for the Central Powers as it was on the Western Front. In Italy the Italians had recovered from Caporetto and gained a victory for the Entente at the battle of Megiddo, that caused the Ottoman Empire to withdraw from the war. Allenby's Entente forces were moving into the defunct Ottoman Empire; and Entente Troops had moved north out of Greece through Serbia, into Austria Hungry. Bulgaria and Romania. What was driving the German Generals' request for a cease fire was that the Entente Troops faced serious pressure on all fronts and that a cease fire was the only way to get some advantages with the troops that were holding those fronts.

Chapter 20
The Treaty of Versailles and the Great Depression

20.1 Peace for Vultures

In June of 1919 the Entente and Central Powers sent representatives to Versailles to begin to work out the details of a peace treaty that would end the war. After several months of heated discussion, they were able to draft what became the Treaty of Versailles, which would be signed by representatives from Great Britain, France, and the United States. The Germans were not invited to even see the final draft of the treaty until it had been completed. A council of three Entente Leaders, consisting of Woodrow Wilson of the United States, David Lloyd George of Great Britain, and Georges Clemenceau of France were the supervising voices in the negotiations that could end the war, and they had very little interest in a continued involvement with the territories created by the destruction of empires.

The cost of the war left all the countries involved in the war had problems controlling prices during and just after the war ended. Figure 20.1 shows the index of prices in the major powers from 1914 through 1925.

The British had managed to stem the inflationary increase in prices by 1920 and were able to maintain stable price indices. The French elected to pursue a policy that slowed the increase in wartime prices, but they made no attempt to return to the antebellum level of prices. The Austrian and Russian economies eventually collapsed under the weight of hyperinflation by the end of 1917, while the newly created Weimar Republic of Germany inherited a price level four times above the 1913 level, and soon found themselves caught up in an explosion of prices that eventually forced the government to revalue the system of currency in 1924. The economic disruption from inflation in every economy after the war, which is depicted in, was a significant factor shaping the political and economic reorganization of the Weimar Republic that emerged in the wake of wartime defeat.

Much of the blame for the economic and political problems associated with the economic chaos after the war was initially placed on shortcomings in the Treaty of Versailles. In the summer of 1919 John Maynard Keynes, who was part of the British

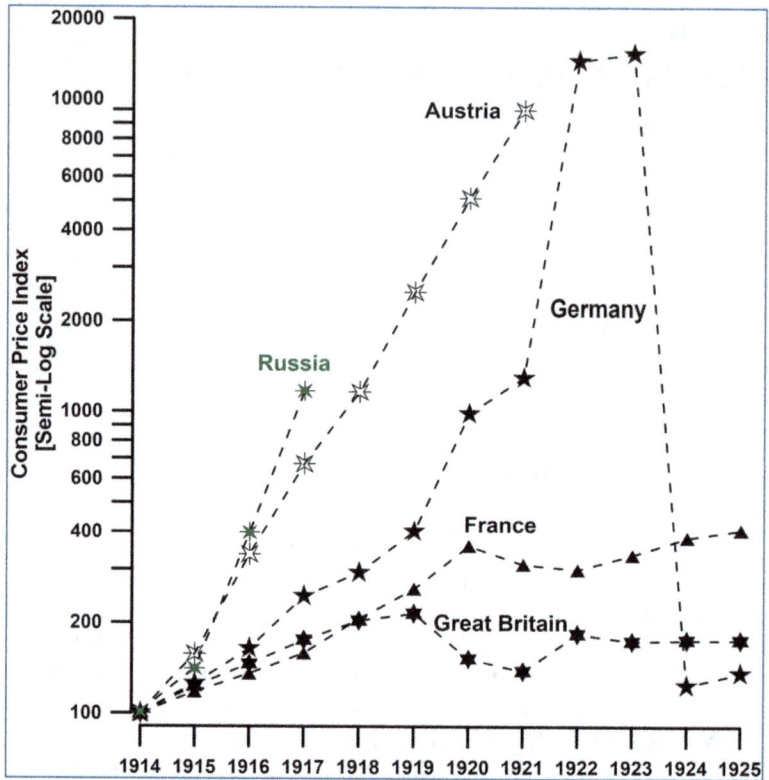

Fig. 20.1 Consumer price indices for five European powers, 1913–1925. *Sources* Wolf (2013), Ransom (2018) and Eichengreen (1992)

delegation to Paris, returned to Britain and wrote a scathing indictment of the treaty and the politicians who were framing it. The treaty, according to Keynes, included

> ... no provisions for the economic rehabilitation of Europe, nothing to make the defeated Central Empires into good neighbors, nothing to stabilize the new States of Europe, nothing to reclaim Russia; nor reached at Paris for restoring the disordered finances of France and Italy, or to adjust the systems of the Old World and the New. (Keynes 1920, 226)

Keynes laid the blame for the shortcomings of the treaty on the narrow attitudes taken by the Council of Four in their deliberations at the Paris Peace Conference. However, the Treaty of Versailles was only the first step in a prolonged process of establishing a peaceful world after 1918. Four additional treaties were signed with the other central powers, and military conflicts involving disputes over borders between the newly formed states of central Europe lasted for another 4 years.[1] Margaret Macmillan points out that the peace makers "could not foresee the future and they certainly could not control it. That was up to their successors. When war came in 1939, it was a result of 20 years of decisions taken or not taken, not of arrangements made in 1919." By 1925 some semblance of economic stability had returned in the form of stable prices in Germany, France, and Great Britain, but the economic disruptions caused by wartime mobilization had dramatically changed the global marketplace. The antebellum financial stability of world trade had rested on the acceptance of a *gold standard* that was the underlying mechanism for the payment of international credits and debts. Currencies were convertible into gold on demand and linked internationally at fixed rates of exchange. Gold shipments were 1 the ultimate means of balance-of-payments settlement. The demise of the Gold Standard and the resulting instability of exchange rates reflected the loss of confidence and the constant fear of unstable markets.[2] In a world fearful of the unknown, the ties that bound the system of global payments were torn apart. An added element of uncertainty in the international capital markets came from the Allied decision to impose reparation payments upon the defeated Germans. After much deliberation the amount demanded was set at 132 billion gold marks, which was divided into three "bond issues" over several years. As events played out, the Germans eventually wound up paying only about 20 billion marks. Most historians have concluded that the impact of the reparation payments was more of a political issue than an economic problem.[3] (Ferguson 1999) Ritschl 2005, Marks 2013). The reparation payments eventually became a political football that was kicked around the Reichstag and Allied governments until Adolf Hitler repudiated the remaining debt in 1933.

All this economic chaos came to a head with the collapse of stock prices on the New York Stock Exchange on October 29, 1929. Figure 20.2 presents the monthly index of the closing value of stocks on the New York Stock Exchange from October 1929 to January 1934. The 36-point decline of the stock index on "Black Thursday" 1929 was the beginning of a downward plummet of stock prices that continued for the next 3 years. By July of 1932 the index of stock prices had fallen to only 12.3% of its value in 1929. The decade of the 1930s was a period of falling commodity prices, declining industrial production and gross domestic products a collapse of world trade, and very high levels of unemployment.

The last major action taken by the Paris Peace Conference was to formulate a comprehensive treaty between the Empire of Germany and the Entente Powers that would not only stop the current war, but would also limit the likelihood of another major war. The German Delegation had not been invited to participate in the discussion of formation of a Comprehensive Peace Treaty. So they did not get to see a copy of the final document until it was presented to them on May 7.

20.2 Woodrow Wilson's Fourteen Points

Led by Wilson, Clemenceau and Lloyd George, the Entente Leaders were determined to break up the coalition that had formed the Central Powers coalition. By 1922 the Russian territory that had been ceded to Germany by the Treaty of Brest-Litovsk had been returned into states that existed before the war: Latvia, Lithuania, Poland, Czechoslovakia, and Romania. North Schleswig was returned to Denmark, and Alsace-Lorraine was returned to France. A portion of the Rhineland along Germany's

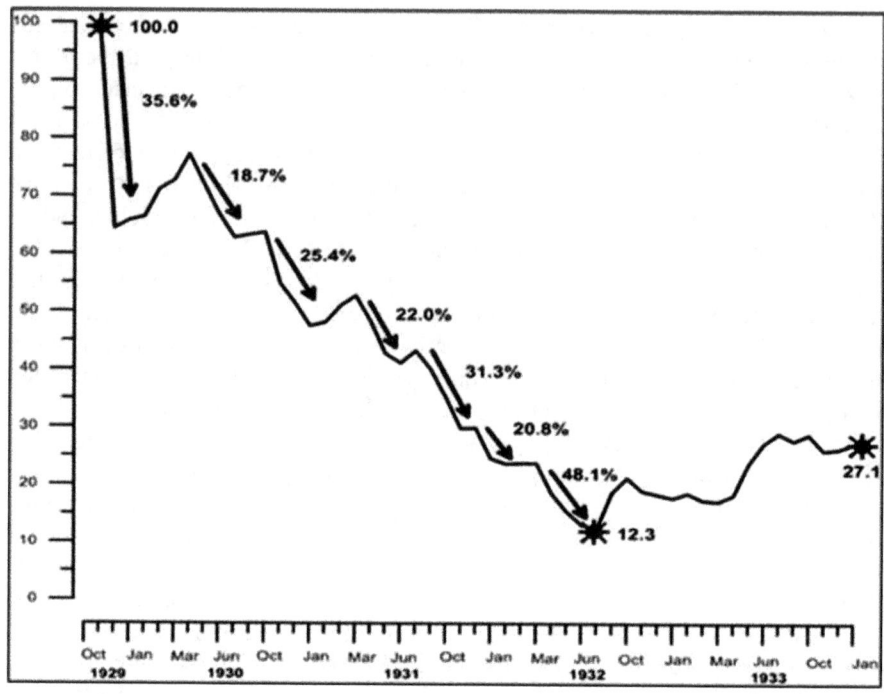

Fig. 20.2 The great stock market crash. *Sources* Wolf (2013), Ransom (2018) and Eichengreen (1992)

western border was declared to be a "demilitarized zone" where no German military forces or fortifications were permitted. As a further limit to German's military abilities, her army was limited to 100,000 men; she could not have an air force, and the navy was limited to 15,000 men and prohibited to have submarines.

On January 18, 1917, the American President Woodrow Wilson delivered what became known as his "14 Points" speech to the U.S. Senate. On April 2nd he asked Congress to approve a vote to declare War on Germany, and two days later Congress approved his request.

Woodrow Wilson's 14 Points

1. Open covenants of peace, openly arrived at, after which there shall be no private international understandings of any kind but diplomacy shall proceed always frankly and in the public view.
2. Absolute freedom of navigation upon the seas, outside territorial waters, alike in peace and in war, except as the seas may be closed in whole or in part by international action for the enforcement of international covenants.

20.2 Woodrow Wilson's Fourteen Points

3. The removal, so far as possible, of all economic barriers and the establishment of an equality of trade conditions among all the nations consenting to the peace and associating themselves for its maintenance.
4. Adequate guarantees given and taken that national armaments will be reduced to the lowest point consistent with domestic safety.
5. A free, open-minded, and absolutely impartial adjustment of all colonial claims, based upon a strict observance of the principle that in determining all such questions of sovereignty the interests of the populations concerned must have equal weight with the equitable claims of the government whose title is to be determined.
6. The evacuation of all Russian territory and such a settlement of all questions affecting Russia as will secure the best and freest cooperation of the other nations of the world in obtaining for her an unhampered and unembarrassed opportunity for the independent determination of her own political development and national policy and assure her of a sincere welcome into the society of free nations under institutions of her own choosing; and, more than a welcome, assistance also of every kind that she may need and may herself desire. The treatment accorded Russia by her sister nations in the months to come will be the acid test of their good will, of their comprehension of her needs as distinguished from their own interests, and of their intelligent and unselfish sympathy.
7. Belgium, the whole world will agree, must be evacuated and restored, without any attempt to limit the sovereignty which she enjoys in common with all other free nations. No other single act will serve as this will serve to restore confidence among the nations in the laws which they have themselves set and determined for the government of their relations with one another. Without this healing act the whole structure and validity of international law is forever impaired.
8. All French territory should be freed and the invaded portions restored, and the wrong done to France by Prussia in 1871 in the matter of Alsace-Lorraine, which has unsettled the peace of the world for nearly fifty years, should be righted, in order that peace may once more be made secure in the interest of all.
9. A readjustment of the frontiers of Italy should be effected along clearly recognizable lines of nationality.
10. The peoples of Austria-Hungary, whose place among the nations we wish to see safeguarded and assured, should be accorded the freest opportunity to autonomous development.
11. Rumania, Serbia, and Montenegro should be evacuated; occupied territories restored; Serbia accorded free and secure access to the sea; and the relations of the several Balkan states to one another determined by friendly counsel along historically established lines of allegiance and nationality; and international guarantees of the political and economic independence and territorial integrity of the several Balkan states should be entered into.
12. The Turkish portion of the present Ottoman Empire should be assured a secure sovereignty, but the other nationalities which are now under Turkish rule should be assured an undoubted security of life and an absolutely unmolested opportunity of autonomous development, and the Dardanelles should be permanently opened as a free passage to the ships and commerce of all nations under international guarantees.

> 13. An independent Polish state should be erected which should include the territories inhabited by indisputably Polish populations, which should be assured a free and secure access to the sea, and whose political and economic independence and territorial integrity should be guaranteed by international covenant.
> 14. A general association of nations must be formed under specific covenants for the purpose of affording mutual guarantees of political independence and territorial integrity to great and small states alike.

Having made what would become the cornerstone for the American team's positions for the Conference, the president took off for the meeting of the Paris Peace Conference, stopping at London. Before he got to Paris Wilson gave several speeches to enthusiastic crowds.

Many of these points were implemented successfully. Austria-Hungary had its territories taken away and formed into free states. Alsace-Lorraine was returned to the French and Poland was created and guaranteed access to the Sea. However, what might appear on the surface to be a successful meeting of imperialist demands for new borders had many cracks if inspected more closely. While a League of Nations was created by the Paris Peace group, the American Congress prevented the United States from joining it because they felt joining the League was giving away American sovereignty in the exercise of world policy. The lack of American support combined with the general fatigue of European powers exhausted by years of war meant that the League of Nations was never able to properly fulfill its role as a deterrent to further imperialism. In fact, many of the nations included in the league had not fully relinquished their imperial ambitions for the war, they had just resigned to not extending those ambitions to Europe.

One of the more significant results from the creation of new state boundaries created by the Treaty of Versailles was the breakup of the Ottoman Empire. The occupation of Constantinople by British, and Italian troops in November of 1918 produced a partitioning of the Ottoman Empire into a conglomeration of new states, following in general the guidelines of the Sykes-Picot Map of 1916. Figure 19.3 shows the new states that were created: Austria, Czechoslovakia, Hungary, Poland, Romania, and Yugoslavia (Fig. 20.3).

Wilson's 14 points offered a whole new menu of issues that needed to be dealt with to constitute a workable peace after the fighting stopped. On the surface they argued this was an anti-imperialist effort since the French and British "liberated" these nations from the Ottoman Empire. However, many of these nations were only released as Mandates of Britain or France. This meant that rather than true freedom they were now being administered by the British and French Colonial Departments instead of the defunct Ottoman Empire.

Among the many nations included in this change of administration was British Palestine. A declaration by British General Arthur Balfour in November of 1917, after Britain had taken Palestine from the Ottoman Empire, the British government gave support to the creation of a new Jewish only state within these new territories. This declaration is often cited as creating greater support within Britain for the creation

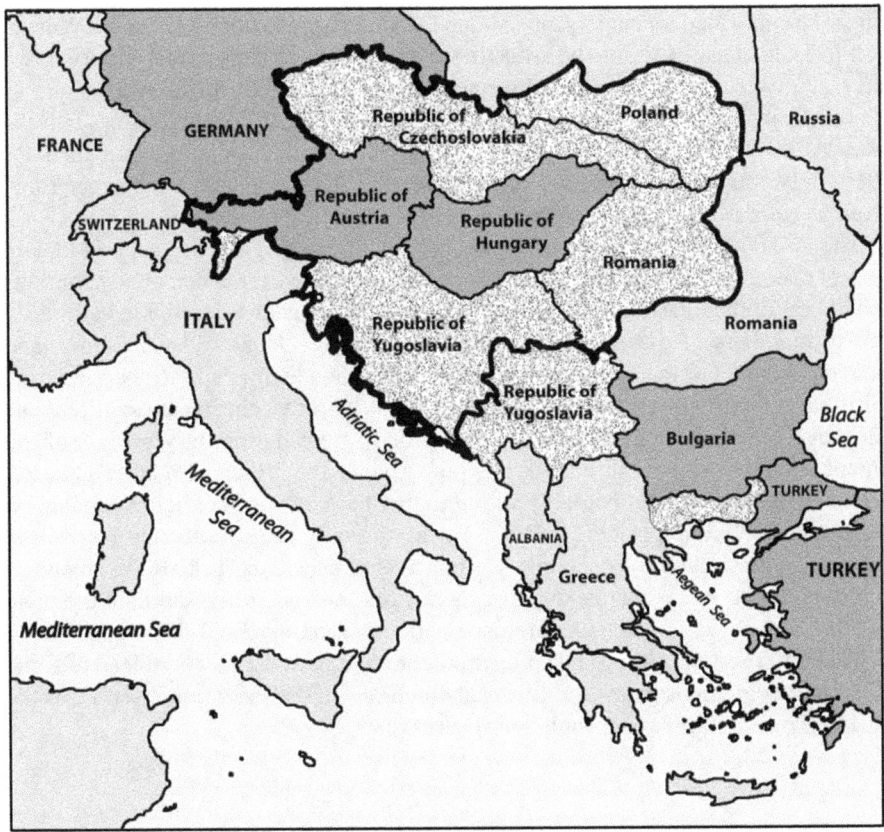

Fig. 20.3 The breakup of the Austrian Hungarian empire. *Sources* Ransom (2018), MacMillan (2001) and Henig (1995)

of a Zionist state and it helped lead to the development of Israel under the incoming British mandate.

20.3 The Italians and the Japanese Go Home with Their Imperial Appetites Unsated

America was happy to play the peacemaker and Britain and France were pleased with their treaties in the middle east. But not every Entente Power at the Paris Peace Conference was satisfied with how the spoils of the war were distributed. Vittorio Orlando was the head of the Italian delegation to the Conference. His principal goal for the treaty was obtaining a region to the northeast of Italy that today would be Croatia and Slovenia, that had belonged to the Austrian Empire. Despite his best efforts he was foiled repeatedly, most often by American President Woodrow Wilson, who insisted this area should be ceded to the new nation of Yugoslavia. Vittorio grew increasingly frustrated with the Wilson's continual denial of his ambitions and as the increasing diplomatic frictions began to undermine Italy's relationship with the other Allies he decided to give up and resigned from the conference on June 19, 1919. Italy was left to feel rather bitter about their lack of gains in the peace time, given he promises they had received in 1914.

The up-and-coming Empire of Japan also felt slighted. They had aspired to gain control over all of Germany's pacific island colonies, however. when all the comings and goings of the treaties were completed, the pacific Islands were divided primarily among members of the British commonwealth. While Japan did gain some land from the former German Empire, it was much less than their newly formed Imperial spirit had them feeling they deserved. It did not help that the Japanese diplomats felt that they were being overlooked or excluded from the primary powers of the Entente. When a Japanese clause was put to vote, the "Racial Equality Clause," President Wilson would invariably veto it under the pretext of not being voted upon unanimously. One might note that these were the only times in the entirety of the conference that unanimous support was considered necessary. Like Italy, Japan felt that the Entente Allies were excluding them from the real conversation at the table and they came away from the conference with bitter memories of their time there.

This bitterness was left to fester over the interwar period and would lead to some of the more egregious growth of Imperial ambitions in the short time to come as the Entente Powers fumbled through their peace treaty.

20.4 Fallout Treaties

Perhaps it is unsurprising that a conference that would leave so many feelings excluded would result in a shorter period of smaller conflicts and quick treaties. For example, the Treaty of Sevres, signed on August 10, 1920, was made to further dismantle the Ottoman Empire. The agreement was supposed to cede Constantinople to Greece. However, rather than handing it over, the treaty makers quickly drummed up Turkish nationalism and the Turkish Signatories of the treaty were stripped of their Citizenship and berated. After 2 years of conflict between Greece and Turkey there was once again a peace conference, resulting in the treaty of Lausanne Signed on July 1923. This replaced the Treaty of Sevres, resulting in the formation of the Turkish Republic.

Notes

1. The other treaties were:
    The *Treaty of Saint-Germaine-en-Laye*, signed with Austria on September 10, 1919;
    The *Treaty of Neuilly-sur Seine* with Bulgaria on November 27, 1919;
    The *Treaty of Trianon* signed with Hungary on June 4, 1920.
    The *Treaty of Sèvres* with the Ottoman Empire on August10, 1920.
    For more on these treaties see (Henig 1995, Boemeke et al. 1998, Ransom 2018).
2. For more on the loss of confidence associated with the problem of exchange rates and the gold standard see Eichengreen and Temin (1997), Eichengreen (1992), Eichengreen (1991) Ransom (2018), Findlay and O'Rourke (2007) and Wolf (2013).
3. MacMillan (2001, 493–4). MacMillan's book is one of the best summaries of the Paris Peace Conference and the Treaty of Versailles.

Chapter 21
Adolf Hitler and the Rise of National Socialism

21.1 Adolf Hitler and the Beer Hall Putsch

On November 8, 1923, former general Erich Ludendorff, who was a hero of the First World War, and the 34-year-old Adolf Hitler, who was head of the newly formed Nazi Political Party, led approximately 2000 members of their members to the *Feldherrnhalle*, a Beerhouse in the center of Munich. Their intnet was to organize overthrow of the government of the German Weimar Republic. Their efforts were unsuccessful, and in the mallee surrounding their march, 17 Nazis were killed by government policemen who had surrounded the beerhall. More than 20 of the Nazi leaders were arrested and were subsequently charged of high treason and given light prison sentences from judges who were sympathetic to their cause. Hitler managed to escape immediate arrest, however two days later he was caught and after a trial that lasted 21 days and drew national attention in the press, he was eventually sentenced to serve five years at Landsberg Prison.

21.2 Hitler in Landsberg Prison

Hitler made good use of his time in prison. The court had given him a prison term that allowed him to have frequent meetings in the prison with his Nazi colleagues and also to have colleagues who could visit him in prison to discuss that he could do for the Nazi Party when he was free. "Landsberg," he would tell people, was "my university paid for by the state." Hitler spent much of his time dictating the manuscript of a book he was writing to of his fellow prisoners. The book, which was titled *Mein Kampf, (My Battle)* became a bestseller and solidified Hitler's hold on his leadership in the Nazi party once he was released from prison (Hitler 1918). It remains one of the most important sources for historians studying the rise of the Nazi Party in pre-war Germany.

Hitler's short stay in prison proved to be a major turning point in his efforts to lead the Nazi Party. Among other things, it convinced him that violent demonstrations were not the best way to make the Nazi Party the governing party in the Weimar Republic. From his release from Landsberg Prison on December 20, 1924, to his appointment as Chancellor of Germany in 1933 following a series of electoral victories by the Nazi Party, Hitler was able to use his ability to communicate with large and enthusiastic crowds as a tool for rapid advancement within the Nazi Party leadership. Among the many articles in the Treaty that Hitler adamantly rejected was Article 116, which forced Germany to return of all the territories which were part of the Treaty of Brest-Litovsk to Russia.

21.3 Hitler's Rise to the Head of the Nazi Party

The Nazi party emerged from the 1932 federal elections with 230 seats, which was more than any other party, but not enough to form a government without some help from some other parties in the Reichstag. General Paul von Hindenburg, the hero of the German victories at the battles of Tannenberg in 1914, had defeated Hitler in the presidential election of 1932. However, Hindenburg was unable to form a government that did not include the Nazis, and Hitler refused to serve as the Chancellor of Germany unless he had complete authority to control the government. Because Hitler was enormously popular, leaving him out of the government was not an option. Consequently, at the end of July 1933 Hindenburg reluctantly agreed to appoint Hitler as Chancellor of Germany and the Nazi Party was able to take control of the German Government.

Encouraged by the powers that his new office gave him, Hitler began a systematic program of territorial German expansion. In January 1935 voters in the Saar region of Germany, which had been occupied and governed by the United Kingdom and France from 1920 to 1935 under a League of Nations mandate, voted overwhelmingly to return to German control. No one objected to this proposal, so in 1936 German troops boldly marched into the Rhineland.

Hitler's next target was Austria. Once again, the invasion of German troops was warmly greeted by people currently living in Austria. Hitler then proclaimed an *Anschluss*, which was approved by the German Reichstag on March 13th and ratified by a plebiscite by the Reichstag on April 10, 1938.

Austria was now part of Germany. Hitler could turn his attention to the Sudetenland, a region in the western part of Czechoslovakia which Hitler claimed should be "returned" to Germany. Although the Czech Government was strongly opposed to this proposal of German unification, none of the Western Powers had the courage to challenge Hitler's claim that Czechoslovakia should be part of the German Empire.

With Benito Mussolini's encouragement, Hitler arranged a Hitler's latest effort just outside Munich on September 30, 1938 to consider his latest effort. What emerged from what historians call "The Munigreement of 1938" was a document signed by Mussolini, Hitler, Neville Chamberlain of Britain and Edouard Daladier of France

21.3 Hitler's Rise to the Head of the Nazi Party

stating that the Germans were free to occupy all of Czechoslovakia. In a famous comment that appeared in all the London Newspapers, Neville Chamberlian is shown getting off the plane from Munich waving a piece of paper and shouting "It is peace for our time" (Fig. 21.1).

Table 21.1 shows that in 1933 Germany's army was limited to 115,000. By 1940 Hitler that had increased that to 3.3 million men and Military Expenditures had grown from less than 500,000 British Pounds to over 21 million. Pounds of steel and energy production had also increased markedly. As a result of all these increases, and with some support from Benito Musolino and Italy. Italy's contribution to the Central Power Allies CINC can be seen in Table 21.1

Hitler encouraged by his victories sought going to force the Soviet Union to return the Russian territory given Germany by the Treaty of Brest-Litovsk in March of 1918 and then taken away by the Treaty of Versailles in 1919. Believing after his success with the Anschluss and the invasion of France that taking over the Soviets to his east would be an easy affair.

He was wrong, of course.

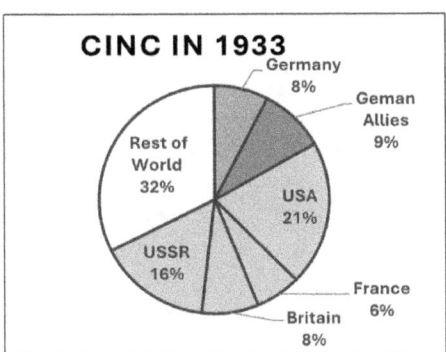
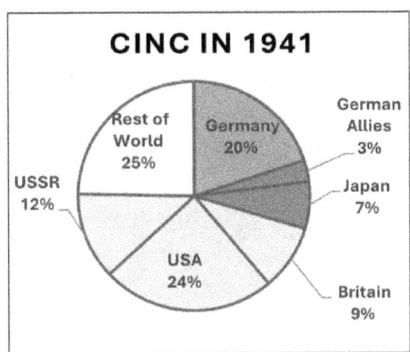

Fig. 21.1 The global distribution of CINC in 1933 and 1941. *Source* Singer and the correlates of war project at https://correlatesofwar.org/

Table 21.1 German CINC: 1933–1940

Year	MILEX	MILPER	IRST	PEC	CINC	%CINC
1933	452,198	118	7617	142,316	0.0777	7.77
1934	709,088	315	11,923	159,244	0.0891	8.91
1935	1,607,587	461	16,447	176,974	0.1026	10.26
1936	2,332,782	596	19,208	190,767	0.1151	11.51
1937	3,298,869	603	19,849	213,420	0.1179	11.79
1938	7,415,163	782	22,656	232,155	0.1542	15.42
1939	12,000,000	2750	23,733	255,050	0.1780	17.80
1940	21,200,000	3300	21,540	256,916	0.1714	17.14

Chapter 22
Operation Barbarossa

22.1 A New Age of Warfare

In the first World War battles were fought across mostly static lines. Accented by desperate pushes that cost thousands of lives for each mile crawled forward into enemy territory. Technologies such as the trench and artillery proved to be highly effective in this type of warfare. The invention of the Tank at the end of the war meant that those established rules would not be the same come the new conflicts at the end of the 1930s.

The new German War doctrine, coined Blitzkrieg, was in many ways the opposite of trench warfare. Rushing forward with fast armored vehicles in order to surround and cut off your enemies. They tested these new military advances both in Poland and Czechoslovakia before they began to plan their assault into the Soviet Union with Operation Barbarossa and their new tactics had proved to be very successful.

The first of many mistakes Hitler would make in his attempted conquest of Russia was to assume that the Soviets would not make as many tanks or tanks of the same quality as German vehicles.

22.2 Josef Stalin and the Soviet Union, 1933–41

On January 21, 1924 Vladimir Lenin passed away. Lenin had been the heart and soul of the Bolshevik victory in the Civil War and his death prompted a spirited scramble among the Bolshevik leaders eager to replace him at the head of the Soviet government. The man who eventually replaced was Joseph Stalin, who was able to use his political position as Lenin's secretary to eventually emerge as the head of the Soviet government (Kotkin 2014; Service 2006).

Stalin had originally been a strong supporter of Lenin's NEP, however the two men gradually drifted apart as Stalin become convinced that even the limited role of market capitalism that was embedded in Lenin's NEP was not well suited for the Soviet Union in a world where all of the major powers were likely to be hostile to the Soviet Union. While Lenin had hoped to integrate the Soviet Union in the global economy, Stalin envisioned a centralized command economy characterized by what he called "Socialism in One Country. His primary objective was to provide economic basis for a military machine to defend the socialist state.

Economic historians have devoted considerable effort to the development of quantitative estimates of economic variables in the Soviet Union in the interwar period. There was virtually no growth in either GDP or population before 1932. Stalin's attempt to reorganize agriculture by collectivized farms was an economic disaster that produced a food crisis that reached the level of a famine in many rural areas during the 1930s (Davies 1980; Davies and Wheatcroft 2004). From a global perspective, the main effect of these policies was to isolate the Soviet Union from the economic and political tensions that were sweeping through Western and Central Europe. (Davies 1989; Davies et al. 2018) For Stalin, all the other powers were potential enemies by 1937. He was determined that the Soviet Union would be ready wherever the next blow might fall.

Despite having a lesser CINC% than Germany during the lead up to operation Barbarossa as shown in Table 22.1, the Soviet's had managed to stay nearly the same in terms of Military Expenditures. Much of these expenditures were spent on expanding and building highly effective Tanks and Artillery for the Soviet Army. Furthermore, these production facilities were built so far east that they could not be reached by German bombers in the event of a war and could continue to faithfully produce Soviet Arms even if Moscow was captured.

To further compound the Soviet advantage the T-34 tank that the Soviets had developed were, in many regards, superior to the German Panzers, especially early into the invasion of Russia. As Historian Victor Davis Hanson Points out,

> Hitler later remarked that had he just been made aware of the nature of Russian tank production, and specifically about the T-34 tank, against which standard German anti-tank weapons were ineffective, he would never have invaded the Soviet Union. (Victor Davis Hanson 2017)

Table 22.1 Soviet Union CINC 1933–1941

	Milex	Milper	IRST	PEC	TOTPOP	UPOP	CINC%
1933	2,363,450	885	6889	96,142	158,168	19,806	15
1934	3,479,651	940	9693	117,627	159,156	22,385	16
1935	5,517,537	1300	12,588	134,681	160,049	25,301	18
1936	2,933,657	1300	16,400	154,026	161,272	28,597	15
1937	3,446,172	1433	17,730	159,512	163,388	32,322	14
1938	5,429,984	1566	18,057	169,211	166,859	36,532	16
1939	5,984,123	1789	17,564	181,115	170,315	35,124	14
1940	6,145,214	4200	18,317	201,846	194,077	33,978	14
1941	6,884,227	4207	15,584	147,154	196,659	32,546	12

Table 22.2 Production of armored military vehicles 1939–1945

	USSR	Germany
1939		700
1940		2200
1941	4800	3800
1942	24,400	6200
1943	24,100	10,700
1944	29,000	18,300
1945	20,500	4,400
Total	102,800	46,300

On top of the superiority of Russian tanks at the time, the Russians simply had more of them. As you can see in Table 22.2 in 1941 when operation Barbarossa begins the Russians produce 1,000 more armored vehicles than the Germans. This number continues to scale as the war continues with The Soviet Union producing at least 20,000 Vehicles a year until the end of the war in 1945. The Germans on the other hand never had a year where they were able to make more than 20,000 tanks.

22.3 Stuck in Stalingrad

By the end of summer 1942, the limits of German territory in the Soviet Union ran in an irregular arc from the outskirts of Leningrad southward to a front just west of Moscow, on South to Voronezh and the west bank of the Don at Stalingrad. It looked as if Hitler might still be able win his great gamble of June 1941. If his armies could anchor the southern end of the occupied area by capturing the city of Stalingrad, Hitler believed he could complete the conquest of the Soviet Union by finishing the attacks on Leningrad and Moscow.

General Friedrich Von Paulus' sixth army reached the city limits of Stalingrad at the end of August 1942. Slowly but surely the Germans fought their way further into the city until, on November 11th von Paulus mounted a final assault that actually reached the Don River. But that would be as far as they would get. The Germans were exhausted, and the Russians had finally regrouped enough men to mount an effective counterattack. Having fought their way into the center of the city, the Germens now found themselves trapped by converging Soviet forces. On November 23rd the Soviet armies linked up west of the city and more than a quarter of a million German soldiers were trapped in the resulting "pocket." On February 2, 1943, von Paulus surrendered his troops.

Stalingrad was a huge victory for the Soviets. The cost of the battle for both sides totaled more than 750,000 men, including prisoners. In addition to the losses inflicted on the Germans, the surrender of an entire army was a huge psychological blow to the Nazis, and had an equally large positive effect on Soviet morale. In addition to relieving the pressure on Stalingrad, the Russian offensive forced the Germans to abandon the Caucuses—which had initially been the main focus of the summer offensives.

22.4 A Third Reich Collapses

The tide of war had inexorably turned against the Axis Powers. Even as the Soviet Union began the slow work of pushing the Germans out of Occupied Russia and later Poland. Their western allies, the British and the Americans primarily, began to plan a naval invasion operation to liberate Vichy France. On June 6, 1944 operation D Day began and despite massive losses the Allies were successful in their invasion. Two months later on August 25, 1944, Paris was liberated and Nazi Germany was surrounded by enemies closing in.

Safely tucked away in a bunker at Berlin with his wife Ava Brown Hitler saw the writing on the wall and made a quick exit with a bullet to the brain on April 30, 1945. His Successor via his will Karl Dönitz, stepped in as ruler of the Third Reich and quickly organized it's surrender to the allied powers. Thus ending operation Barbarossa.

Chapter 23
Dreams of a Rising Sun

23.1 A Rising Japan

While Hitler was bringing Germany back as a major military power, a new imperial power was emerging in the Orient. Until halfway through the nineteenth century the Japanese practiced total Isolationism. They were completely cut off from the rest of the world as the industrial revolution rapidly changed how quickly and efficiently people were able to manufacture goods. Japan remained totally free from this rapid industrialism. Shortly after commodore Matthew Perry disrupted Japan's Isolationist policy in 1853 with a show of military force and advanced technology a collection of Japanese nobles and samurai placed the young Emperor Meiji on the throne. In what would come to be known as the 1868 Meiji restoration, Japan began a process of rapid industrialization. Making use of their ample supply of silk, which was in great demand by European and American markets, they began actively trading in European markets and used the exchange earned in those markets to for cover the costs of building factories and infrastructure in their own markets. At the same time, impressed by what they had seen from the Americans, they began to copy the military structure of the Western Powers. From 1868 to 1890 Japan's Urban population doubled, the amount of Iron and steel they produced increased tenfold, and they went from no coal power to 8000 tons of coal worth of energy a year. When the twentieth century rolled around, Japan's performance against Russia in Manchuria had firmly established itself as a growing industrial power. Unfortunately for Japan, industry can only grow so long as the resources are there to support it. Japan, as an island nation, turned its eyes outwards in search of territories that could support their industrial sector.

We have already dealt with the Russo-Japanese war in Chapter 14 and seen that Japan's imperial ambition did not end with the taking of Korea. Still simmering after what they felt was an unfair rebuttal by the Entente Council members in the deliberations of the Paris Peace Talks of Versailles, Japan began to plot on how to expand their interests throughout the Pacific. By 1931 Japanese Military officers finally grew fed up with the impassive state of their empire and hatched a plot to gain *Casus Belli* for a further invasion of Manchuria. A large section of railway was mysteriously blown away on the 18th of September. Not one to let such a situation go lightly, the Japanese quickly pinned the issue on Chinese nationalists and sent troops to invade Manchuria. In what became known as the Mukden incident, the untrained Chinese Army posed very little resistance to the eager and ready Japanese troops who quickly conquered much of the area. The Japanese renamed the area Manchukuo, and it became an autonomous state that was totally controlled by the Japanese Army. Outward eyes saw this happen, but the rapid collapse of Manchuria, combined with the internal pains of a global depression in the 1930s meant that neither the former entente states or the league of nations were able to do much of anything but offer too late condemnations.

Still, Japan's Imperial ambitions were not satiated, and they continued to push their interests into southern Mongolia, which they eventually formed into the autonomous zone of Mengjiang. Combined with taking control of islands around Japan that had been an ongoing effort of the empire since they began their industrialization, by 1936 Japan had all the makings of an imperial empire looking to establish itself as a hegemonic power that needed to be respected around the world (Fig. 23.1).

23.2 Ambitions Burning Too Bright

A series of quick and successful wars had convinced the Japanese people of their military confidence and inspired a great deal of nationalism. Their ambitions grew proportionally, in the same way that Adolf Hitler's dream of Lebensraum served as a strong incentive to expand the German Empire, the Japanese were creating a plan of imperial expansion that they called the *Greater East Asian Co-Prosperity Sphere*. This consisted of organizing a unified bloc of Pacific nations that would be under Japanese control and would be totally self-sufficient and separate from European influences.

It did not take much rumination on the part of Japan to realize that there were several obstacles to these imperialistic goals; the chief among them being the United States, who had been expanding their own interests in the Pacific Islands. A growing number of Japanese military officers—particularly the commanders in the Imperial Japanese Navy [IJN]—felt that a pre-emptive strike to cripple the American Navy was necessary to protect their interests in the Southeast Pacific. The argument for a quick and decisive war, a shattering of American Navy that would push the Americans out of the pacific and towards isolationism was spearheaded by the commander in chief of the Imperial Japanese Navy's Combined Fleet, Admiral Isoroku Yamamoto.

The Combined Fleet was the sea-going component of the Imperial Japanese Navy. Known as *Kido Butai*, it was an attack force that included a total of 31 ships in all, including all six of Japan's aircraft carriers, two battleships, two heavy cruisers, and nine of the navy's newest destroyers. What the Japanese navy had created with *Kido Butai* was equivalent to what the Germans had created with their Panzer Corps on

23.2 Ambitions Burning Too Bright

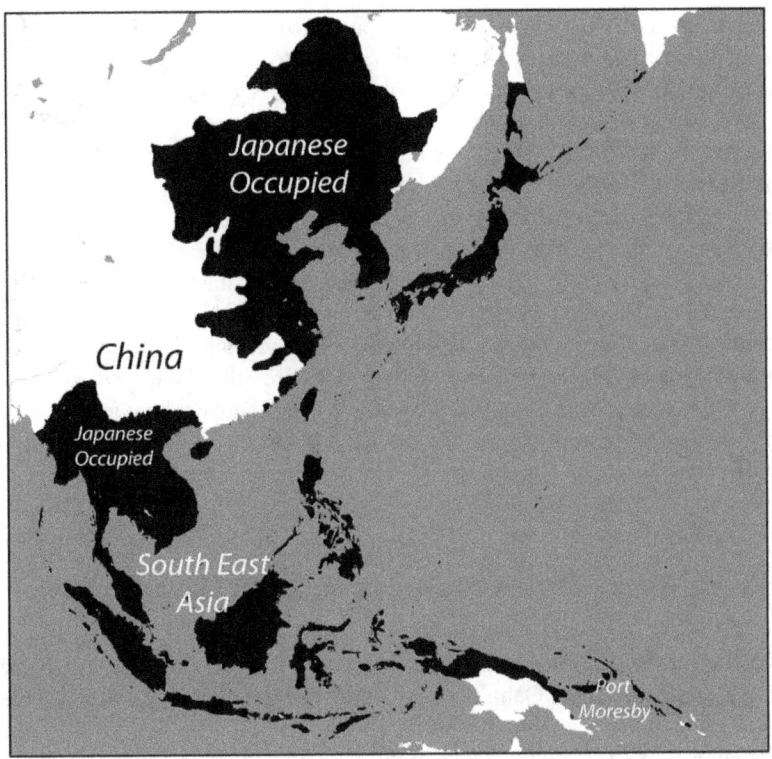

Fig. 23.1 The Japanese empire in 1941. *Sources* Tyler (1905), Ransom (2018), Clodfelter (2015) and Hanson (2017)

land: it was a strike force with offensive power that was unmatched by any other fleet in the world. Yamamoto believed that a surprise attack on the American fleet at Pearl Harbor would send a message to the Americans to not interfere with the Japanese interests in the Pacific, and the sooner the Japanese launched an attack, the better.

"The presence of the US fleet in Hawaii," he pointed out, "is a dagger pointed at our throats. Should war be declared the length and breadth of our southern operation would immediately be exposed to serious threat orders point" (Potter 1967, 84). In August 1940, when Yamamoto first presented his plan to have the IJN attack the American fleet at Pearl Harbor to the Naval High Command the idea was not well-received. However, Yamamoto's arguments that the IJN must take the offensive received a boost from the course of diplomatic and economic events. The existing plan was that the IJN would sit behind a screen of islands in the Western Pacific and lure the Americans into a huge defensive battle. Yamamoto argued that this would not protect the Japanese forces in east Asia.

In the Spring of 1941 Yamamoto's arguments that the IJN must take offensive action against the Americans received a boost from the course of diplomatic and economic events facing Japan. For some time, the U.S. government had imposed an embargo against American exports to Japan. Dwindling supplies of gasoline and oil in Japan were becoming critical, and Yamamoto was convinced that time was running out for the Japanese to take control of territories that could supply these vital inputs. The extent of the shortage was explained to the emperor for the first time. By early November 1940—before the emperor had even heard of the plan to attack the American Pacific Fleet at Pearl Harbor—Yamamoto was making preparations for the Combined Fleet to rendezvous at Tankan Bay, a remote spot in the Kurile Islands, to refuel and prepare to launch an attack on Hawaii. By the time Emperor Hirohito had actually signed the order authorizing the attack, the IJN carrier force had already set sail for its target. It was an impressive armada: a total of 31 ships in all, including six carriers, two battleships, two heavy cruisers, and nine of Japan's newest destroyers. With their combined fleet task force the Japanese had created an offensive weapon that was unmatched by any fleet in the world navies.[1]

And now they were about to use it to attack the American fleet that was harbored at Pearl Harbor.

23.3 Tora, Tora, Tora: The Attack on Pearl Harbor

At 6 o'clock on the morning of December 7, 1941 the *Kido Buta* attack force was situated 230 miles north of Oahu and the American fleet anchored at Pearl Harbor. With the code words *Tora, Tora, Tora* echoing in their ears, more than 180 Japanese bomber planes took off from the decks of the *Kido Buta* carriers and headed for Pearl Harbor. Guided by the signal of a radio station in Honolulu, the planes raced towards their target. When American spotters first spotted the planes coming into range of their equipment, they mistook them for a flight of American B-17 Bombers coming in from the mainland. They were wrong. The planes were IJN airplanes that were carrying out a bombing attack of Pearl Harbor from the decks of *Kido Butia*. Within two hours Pearl Harbor had been turned into a burning inferno. Eight battleships, three cruisers, and three destroyers were either sunk or seriously damaged by attacks from the Japanese aircraft that had been launched from ships that were distance of more than a hundred miles away.

The attack on Pearl Harbor was an example of ingenious military planning on a grand scale. But, as British historian John Keegan noted "it was no Trafalgar" (Keegan 1989, 255). It was certainly a "wake-up" call that brought the Americans into the war with Japan. But the results of the attack did not provide the damage to the American battle fleet that Yamamoto needed for his larger plan to block the western expansion of the American Navy. It is true that all eight American battleships that were docked at Pearl Harbor were seriously damaged. However, all but one of those battle ships—the *Arizona*—were repaired before the end of the war and saw action later in the Pacific War.[2] "Dreadnaughts" were no longer the heart of naval fleets. *Kido Butia* did not use battleships to attack Pearl Harbor; they used aircraft carriers that could launch dozens of planes to attack enemy targets that were still out of sight.

For the next five months the Japanese and American Navies struggled to find each other somewhere in the Pacific Ocean.

23.4 The Dolittle Raids

Americans took it upon themselves to find a way to retaliate against Japan with their own carriers in the same manner as the attack on used on Pearl Harbor. In January of 1942 Navy Captain Francis S. Low, who was a submarine officer on the staff of the Chief of Naval Operations when war broke out, came up with a novel idea to shake the confidence of the Japanese Home Defenses. Low insisted that a B-25 bomber could be modified to take off from an aircraft carrier. He suggested that the Navy should get their aircraft carriers close enough to Japan that they could launch a strike of B-25's over Japanese cities—including Tokyo. "Jimmy" Dolittle, a well-known test pilot at the time, was assigned to plan the operation. What followed was months of testing and modifying B-25 bombers to operate from an aircraft carrier and negotiating with China to allow for landing and refueling for the trip back. It was not until April 18th, 1942, that 25 of the modified B-25's could finally take off from USS Hornet and headed for various targets in the Japanese homeland.

Physically the "Dolittle Raid" of B-25's did not significantly disrupt Japanese Industry or military preparation. Psychologically however, the effect was a major accomplishment. This was the first time since the Japanese had started their imperial wars that damage had been inflicted upon the Japanese mainland by an enemy power. Regardless of whether it was truly effective or not, Japanese planners had to start worrying as the new American threat to bomb the home island ramped up. Yamamoto could no longer able to be content with the back and forth of the Pacific Ocean Cat and Mouse game.

23.5 Battle at the Coral Sea

The Japanese were not the only navy that had aircraft carriers. Both the British and the American Navies had carrier fleets in the Atlantic, and the Americans had a Pacific Carrier Fleet that included three aircraft carriers: *Enterprise*, *Yorktown*, and *Hornet*. None of these ships were docked at Pearl Harbor, which meant that although the attack on Pearl Harbor had sunk or crippled the U.S. Navy's fleet of battleships, the Americans were still in a position to attack the Japanese Fleet with its own fleet of aircraft carriers. Shortly after the Dolittle Raids, the Japanese and American Navies—both eager to prove they could defend their homeland and secure their presence in the Pacific—clashed over a period of four days as Japan tried to secure Port Moresby to secure the southern border of their empire. In what would become known as the Battle of the Coral Sea, American and Japanese aircraft carriers staged a battle in which the contesting ships never saw each other. All of the action was carried out with airplanes attacking enemy ships. Besides the aircraft carriers, no other naval vessel was able to inflict any amount of damage on the opposing fleets, because the fleets kept hundreds of miles between each other as they sent fleets of aircraft to attack the opposing fleet. The Americans lost the USS *Lexington,* and the USS *Yorktown* was heavily damaged. The Japanese lost the light carrier and had the fleet carrier significantly damaged. The Japanese loss was probably greater than the American loss, since they could have used the *Shoho* at Battle of Midway,

Notes

1. For more on the development of the IJN *Kido Butai* attack group as a powerful new weapon and strategy using aircraft carriers, see the discussions in Thomas (2006) and Potter (1967).
2. The Arizona was left where she sank during the attack in shallow water, and she still serves as a monument to the Pearl Harbor Attack.

Chapter 24
The Battle of Midway

24.1 The Battle of Midway

What Yamamoto wanted was a battle between the two fleets and their aircraft carriers somewhere in the Pacific Ocean north of Hawaii that would decide who would be in control of the Pacific theater of the war. After the attack on Pearl Harbor, Yamamoto moved the Japanese fleet northward from Hawaii towards Midway Island, which is a tiny atoll situated in the middle of the Pacific Ocean halfway between Japan and the coast of California. In the summer of 1942 Midway Island and Wake Island were serving as islands that were acting as important lookouts for the American Navy to keep track of the activity of the Japanese naval forces. Neither side knew exactly where the other's carrier fleets were located, and Yamamoto hoped to surprise the Americans. He chose Midway Island and Wake Island as the best places to lie in wait for the Americans to expose their position for a surprise attack. However, the Americans had intercepted a coded Japanese message that clearly identified Wake Island as the place where the *Kido Buai* was waiting for the American aircraft carriers to arrive.[1]

But it would be the Japanese carriers, not the Americans who were surprised. Early in the morning of June 4th American scout planes had found *Kido Buai* and Admiral Chester Nimitz, Commander of the U.S. Pacific Fleet, immediately ordered a contingent of dive bombers from two American carriers—the USS *Enterprise* and USS *Yorktown*—to launch a major attack against the *Kido Bai*.

When Japanese scout planes brought news of the approaching American attack bombers, Japanese Vice Admiral Chūichi Nagumo—who was directing the re-arming of Japanese planes for a bombing raid on Wake Island—ordered that the ordnance on those planes be changed to deal with the approaching American bombers. Unfortunately for the Japanese, their flight crews were still in the process of changing ordinance for the Japanese fighter planes on the deck of their carriers when the American planes arrived on the scene. Without any opposition from Japanese fighters, the American pilots were free to attack the Japanese carriers with their bombs. To make things worse for the Japanese, the decision to change armaments at the last moment meant that bombs and other ordinance meant for the Japanese planes were scattered on the Japanese carrier decks. The explosions of loose pieces of ordinance that were hit by exploding American bombs added to the damage from bombs as they hit the carrier Japanese decks.

The result of all this confusion in the Japanese fleet was that the American planes were able to sink three Japanese carriers: *Akagi, Kaga, and Soryu*, and they damaged a fourth carrier, *Hiryu*, badly enough that the Japanese had to scuttle the ship the following day. The Japanese heavy cruiser Mikuma was also sunk by the American planes. The Japanese got some small level of satisfaction the following day when one of their submarines managed to finally sink the damaged USS *Yorktown*. However, this hardly balanced the loss of four of their best aircraft carriers, together with the 3.000 casualties that included over 300 experienced pilots that were lost in the battle.

> The Battle of Midway was a crushing defeat for the Imperial Japanese Navy. They still had several fleet carriers that were available for action, but they were be able to replace only one of the carriers they lost at Midway. By contrast, Americans were able to produce five new Essex class carriers to add to their Pacific Fleet by the end of the war.

By mid-1942 Japan had been able to expand their Asian empire to control a large part of the East coast of China and they had secured a group of islands that extended in a wide arc through the South Pacific stopping just short of Port Moresby. The Americans could choose between engaging to engaging the Japanese forces in China, or they could launch a series of offensive attacks that would capture the Japanese garrisons located on islands between Port Moresby and the Japanese mainland.

24.2 Island Hoping and the DUKW Landing Crafts

With General Douglas MacArthur in command of the Army and Admiral Chester Nimitz in charge of the Navy, the Americans were able to develop a strategy that became known as *Island Hopping*. The two commanders would choose to attack islands where the Japanese had established some level of defense. They tended to avoid the larger islands and concentrate their efforts to occupy smaller outposts with airfields that gradually brought American forces closer to the Japanese home Islands. By the spring of 1942 the American Navy had worked out a systematic procedure for attacking the Japanese islands. Battle ships would bombard the target island with their heavy batteries. Marines would then land on the beach with the assistance of amphibious vehicles that were called DUKW's. These were specially designed amphibious mini-tanks with light armor and specially designed apparatus for the landing of troops on the unpredictable terrain of the island beaches. These boat-trucks with wheels looked a little awkward. But their weird design allowed troops to drive them directly from water onto the beach, which was a crucially important task, since beach-hopping involved a series of invasions against enemy-held Beaches, large ships were forced to sail up to the shore for the time-consuming process of unloading men and equipment. DUKW's simplified this because they were pre-loaded vehicles that drove right out of a ship, across a few miles of water and onto the sand. They were Army vehicles that truck drivers trained to use as land trucks, and they were very useful, especially with their added ability to transition from land to river travel.

Following the stunning victory at Midway, the American commanders agreed that the next objective for the American forces would be to keep the Japanese from occupying Port Moresby and the Island of Guadalcanal. On August 7, 1942, a division of American marines landed on Guadalcanal, marking the beginning of the first American land offensive of the Pacific War. The Guadalcanal landings initially met little resistance, however heavy fighting soon spread to neighboring islands and continued for several months, with the Japanese eventually withdrawing from the island in February of 1943.

> Island-hopping introduced a new set of requirements for the marine units. The tides could be very unpredictable, and the enemy was dug into their hillside defenses. Rear Admiral Keiji Shibasaki, the commander of the Japanese forces on Tarawa Island, claimed it would take a million Americans a hundred years to breakthrough their defenses. A force of American Marines took the Island in three days, however the battle revealed the danger and frustration of fighting this sort of a war. The Marines were often forced to wade 100 meters or more through the surf to make it to shore; all the while under enemy fire. Luckily for the Americans. Tarawa was the bloodiest example of this form of warfare in the Island-Hopping Campaign. Further island invasions were easier both because of technological advancements such as the DUKW's and because more secure supply lines opened had been up as the marines took more islands.

24.3 The Manhattan Project and the Trinity Test

On December 28, 1942, President Franklyn Roosevelt authorized the formation of an agency to supervise the government's efforts to develop nuclear weapons. Roosevelt's action was a response to fears that Nazi scientists were working to develop a nuclear weapon. Because its office was initially located in New York, and the activities of the agency were conducted at the highest level of secrecy, it became known as *The Manhattan Project.* It's research on the possibility of developing an atomic weapon, which was also classified as top secret, was carried out at a research center near Los Banos' New Mexico on December 28, 1942.

As the island hoping strategy brought American forces closer to Japan, the question of what would be the best way to attack the Japanese mainland had become the main interest of American Commanders. Based on the casualties incurred for the recent battles to take the islands of Jima and Okinawa, the best guess for the cost of an invasion of Japan—code named *Operation Downfall*—could possibly exceed 500,000 men. At time when American battle casualties were reaching 65,000 men a month and reinforcements were beginning to get scarce, opening a massive land based offensive to invade Japan did not appeal to any of the American or British high commanders.

While American generals were considering how best to proceed with Operation Downfall, the Manhattan Project scientists were getting ready to test their research into the possibility of building an atomic weapon. Their research indicated that they could use either uranium or plutonium to build a bomb, so they built one of each. The bomb that would use uranium was called "Little Boy"; the bomb that would use plutonium was called "Fat Man." On July 16th, 1945, the Manhattan Project arranged what J. Robert Oppenheimer, the Scientific leader of the Manhattan Project, called the *Trinity Test,* to physically observe the potency of their new weapon. A select group of 424 American scientists, generals, and politicians watched from a dugout ten thousand yards away as a10 ton "Gadget," which was a 20 ton device built to create an explosion equivalent to that of a plutonium "Fat Boy" atomic bomb, was detonated.

The results of the Trinity Test were spectacular. The blast vaporized the 100-foot steel tower it was resting on and turned the sand under the tower into glass. The noise of the explosion could be seen and heard miles away, and a huge mushroom cloud of smoke rose to a height of 40,000feet. Reports from witnesses came from as far as 200 miles away. A forest ranger 150 miles west of the blast said he saw a flash of fire, an explosion, and black smoke. An individual 150 miles north said the explosion "lighted up the sky like the sun." The Manhattan Project observers had a hard time keeping the *Trinity Test* a secret. When a U.S. Navy pilot flying at 10,000 feet near Albuquerque, New Mexico, asked for explanation of the blast, he was simply told, "Don't fly south." After the test, the Alamogordo Air Base issued a press release that stated simply, "A remotely located ammunition magazine containing a considerable number of high explosives and pyrotechnics exploded, but there was no loss of life or limb to anyone."

The actual cause of the blast was not disclosed until after the U.S. bombing of Hiroshima, Japan, on Aug. 6.[2]

24.4 Impact of the Trinity Test

President Truman was in Potsdam, Germany, meeting with British Prime Minister Winston Churchill, Chinese President Chiang Kai-shek, and Soviet Premier Josef Stalin when he got news of the Trinity Test success. Truman was the only leader who got immediate news of the event; the other leaders got the news through their news bureaus.

The demand to surrender was ignored, so America sent their first bomber. On August 6th 1945 a single B-29 Bomber dropped "Little Boy" and set the bomb to detonate one-thousand-nine-hundred and sixty-eight feet above Hiroshima. Ten thousand people were incinerated instantly by the initial blat and many more deaths would follow in the destruction brought about by America's new weapon. Despite this, Japan still did not respond to Truman's earlier demand for surrender. Three days later, on August 9th 1945, the second bomb, "Fat Man" was dropped over Nagasaki. Finally prompting Japan's immediate surrender. The three main points of the surrender of Japan were as follows.

1. Japan shall be permitted to maintain such industries as will sustain her economy and permit the exaction of just reparations in kind, but not those which would enable her to re-arm for war. To this end, access to, as distinguished from control of, raw materials shall be permitted. Eventual Japanese participation in world trade relations shall be permitted.
2. The occupying forces of the Allies shall be withdrawn from Japan as soon as these objectives have been accomplished and there has been established in accordance with the freely expressed will of the Japanese people a peacefully inclined and responsible government.
3. We call upon the government of Japan to proclaim now the unconditional surrender of all Japanese armed forces, and to provide proper and adequate assurances of their good faith in such action. The alternative for Japan is prompt and utter destruction.

Notes

1. There are a collection of books cover the Battle of Midway. Among the most useful is Parsh and Tully (2005).
2. The description of the reaction to the blast is quote is based on a variety of reactions collected by *Wikipedia*.

Chapter 25
Closing

Imperialism has existed in human history for far longer than the 600 years mentioned in our book. The time we have highlighted simply has the most available amount of information for us to pore over and shows a time when empires were not bound to the continent from which they came.

All of these wars in some way or another were born of a nationalistic desire for power and territory, however as we often saw it was rather rare that a nation or empire was able to maintain hold of that territory even when they won the war. If the nation simply sought to obtain economic advantages such as the British East Indian Company in the Mughal Empire they often ended up projecting their power successfully. The British empire was able to levy taxes and resources from India as late as 1947 after the resolution of World War II, but if like the Japanese Empire, Hitler or Napoleon your empire success encouraged you to more reckless wars for the sake of more these land and power the Empire in question would often buckle and fail.

25.1 The Spanish Empire 300 Years of Imperialism

Many of these Imperial ventures were spearheaded by the accomplishments and drive of singular individuals. Cortes and Pizarro are perhaps the most obvious examples before the Second World War. Burning his boats behind him to spur his few men to conquer an empire. They ran a cash register on the isthmus of Panama that ran a business for the merchants of all countries who traded with the "New World" without the need to sail through the straits of Magellan. This meant that much of their gains did not benefit Spain itself but Europe who traded with them. While the results of the Spanish imperialism, little worse than slavery, provided a massive amount of money to the Spanish Empire that was in large part due to the luck of finding gold in the "New World" the power of Spain itself was tied to the extraction of their gold. When the gold ran out the Spanish Empire fell apart but the new economy they had built in Europe remained.

25.2 The American Exception

America exists as a notable outlier to our conclusions. They were one of the few cases where the people being exploited actually won the war and were successfully able to establish themselves. Afterwards they became the most successful imperialists in the world. Much of this is due to their full belief in Manifest Destiny. They fully believed they were owed everything from the corner of Maine to the south of California. Even when these lands were previously inhabited the Americans simply signed into law that the land was American only and forcibly removed the collection of much weaker states and tribes that stood in their way. What they could not buy they found a way to take. Even the uninhabitable Pacific Ocean was not entirely safe from their desire for new territory as Hawaii and the conquests of the Spanish American war meant they put their stamp even there. Notably America is approaching its 300th birthday. It was about 300 years before the Spanish Empire ran out of gold. Perhaps it is simply too early to say that America has been a successful Imperialist.

25.3 The Scared Imperialists

Following the Second World War, the amount and magnitude of Imperial wars saw a noticeable drop. Empires that previously might have pushed their weight around to secure land and power now did so more carefully under the threat of nuclear arms. Wars were fought in the name of political affiliations with different sides backed by different world powers. Rarely was a war fought in the 50 years after the Second World War that could easily be defined as an Imperial War. However, imperialism remains at the center of these conflicts as major powers continue to influence the decisions of smaller nations. More recently, however, some of these nations have started to listen to their greed again and look at their neighbors as a source of income to be taken.

Bibliography

Andrews, Kenneth R. 1984. *Trade, Plunder, and Settlement: Maritime Enterprise and the Genesis of the British Empire. 1480 -1630*. London: Cambridge University Press.
Bauer, K. Jack. 1974. *The Mexican War, 1846–1848*. New York: MacMillan.
Bawlf, Samuel. 2003. *The Secret Voyage of Sir Francis Drake*. London: Walker Books.
Bergreen, Laurence. 1978
Bergreen, Laurence. In Search of a Kingdom: Francis Drake, Elizabeth I, and the Perilous Birth of the British Empire 2021 HarperCollins. Kindle Edition.
Bergreen, Laurence. Over the Edge of the World: Magellan's Terrifying Circumnavigation of the Globe 2003. HarperCollins. Kindle Edition.
Brown, Dee. 2007. *Bury My Heart at Wounded Knee: An Indian History of the American West*. New York: Holt Paperback.
Cameron, Ian. 1973. *Magellan and the first Circumnavigation of the World*. New York: Saturday Review Press.
Cartwright, Mark. 2021. "Spanish Treasure Fleets". *World History Encyclopedia.*
Chrastil, Rachel. 2023. *Bismark's War: The Franco-Prussian War and the Making ot Modern Europe*. New York: Basic Books.
Clodfelter, Micheal. 2015. *Warfare and Armed Conflicts: A Statistical Reference to Casualty and Other Figures, 1500–2000*, 2nd ed. Jefferson, NC: McFarland & Company Inc.
Martin, Colin, and Geoffrey Parker. 2022. *Armada: The Spanish Enterprise and England's Deliverance in 1588*. New Haven: Yale University Press.
Coote, Stephen. 2003. *Drake: The Life and Legend of an Elizabethan Hero*. Â·London: Pocket Books.
Crowley, Roger. 2024. "Spice: The 16th Century Contest That Shaped the Modern World." In. New Haven: Yale University Press.
Dalrymple, William. 2006 The Last Mughal. Knopf Doubleday Publishing Group. Kindle Edition.
Dalrymple, William. 2019 The Anarchy: The East India Company, Corporate Violence, and the Pillage of an Empire (Bloomsbury Publishing. Kindle Edition.
Daniel R. Headrick. 1981. "The Tools of Empire: Technology and European Imperialism in the Nineteenth Century."
Davis, Lance, and Robert Huttenback. 1987. *Mammon and the Pursuit of Empire: The Political Economy of British Imperialism*. New York: Cambridge University Ptess.
Eichengreen, Barry J. 1992. *Golden Fetters: The Gold Standard and the Great Depression, 1919–1939*. New York: Oxford University Press.
Eichengreen, Barry, and Peter Temin. 1997. The Gold Standard and the Great Depression. In *National Bureau of Economic Research: Working Paper 6060*. Cambridge MA.

Eichengreen, Barry. 1991. The Origins and Nature of the Great Slump, Revisited. In *University of California, Berkeley Department of Economics, Working Paper*. Berkeley, CA.

Findlay, Ronald, and Kevin H. O'Rourke. 2007. *Power and Plenty: Trade, War, and the World Economy in the Second Millennium*. Princeton: Princeton University Press.

Fradin, Dennis. 2010. *The Louisiana Purchase*. New York: Marshall Cavendish Benchmark.

Frankopan, Peter. 2015. *The Silk Roads: A New History of the World*. New York: Random House.

Freidel, Frank. 1958. *The Splendid Little War*. Boston: Little Brown and Company.

Golay, Michael. 2003. *The Tide of Empire: Americas's March to the Sea*. Hoboken N J: John Wiley & Sons.

Greenberg, Amy S. 2012a. *Manifest Destiny and American Territorial Expansion*. Boston: Bedford/St.Martins.

Greenberg, Amy. 2012b. *A Wicked War: Polk, Clay, Lincoln and the 1846 U. S. Invasion of Mexico*. Kindle. New York: Alfred Knopf.

Hacker, J. David. 2011. "A Census Based Count the Civil War Dead." *Civil War History* LVII (4).

Hanson, Victor Davis. 2001. "Carnage and Culture: Landmark Battles in the Rise of Western Powers." In: Anchor Books.

Hanson, Victor Davis. 2017 The Second World Wars: How the First Global Conflict Was Fought and Won (pp. 35–36). Basic Books. Kindle Edition.

Henig, Ruth. 1995. *Versailles and After, 1919–1933*, 2nd ed. New York: Routledge.

Hitler, Adolf. 1961. *Hitler's Secret Book*. Translated by Salvator Attanasio. New York: Grove Press.

Hoffman, Philip T. Why Did Europe Conquer the World? (The Princeton Economic History of the Western World Book 54). Princeton University Press. Kindle Edition. 2015

Kotkin, Stephen. 2014 Stalin: Paradoxes of Power, 1878–1928. Penguin Publishing Group. Kindle Edition.

MacMillan, Margaret. 2001. *Paris 1919: Six Months that Changed the World*. New York: Random House.

Boemeke, Manfred, Gerald Feldman, and Elisabeth Glaser, eds. 1998. *The Treaty of Versailles: A Reassessment After 75 Years*. New York: Cambridge University Press.

Mattingly, Garrett. 1963. *The "Invincible" Armada and Elizabethan England*. Amherst Folger Shakespeare Library

McKee, Alexander. 2018. "A World Too Vast: The Four Voyages of Columbus." In. London: Lume Books.

McPherson, 1988 #570

Merk, Frederick. 1963. *Manifest Destiny and Mission in American History*. New York: Vintage.

Merry, Robert W. 2009. *A Country of Vast Designs: James K. Polk, The Mexican War, and the Conquest of the American Continent*. New York: Simon and Schuster.

Morison, Sameul Eliot. 1942. *Admirlal of the Ocean Sea: A Life of Christpher Columbus*. Boston: Little Brown and Company.

Morison, Sameul Eliot. 1978. *The Great Explorers:: The European Discovery of America*. Kindle ed: Oxford University Press.

Newell, Clayton. 2014. "The Regular Army Before the Civil War, 1845–60." In. Washington D.C.: Center for Military History.

Over the Edge of the World: Magellan's Terrifying Circumnavigation of the Globe. Kindle ed. New York: Oxford University Press.

Overy, Richard. 2021. *Blood and Ruins: The Last Imperial War. 1931–1945*. Kindle. London: Penquin Publishing Group.

Palmer, Alan. 1998. *Victory 1918*. New York: Atlantic Monthly Press.

Parshall, Jonathan, and Anthony Tully. 2005. *The Untold Story of the Battle of Midway*. Washington, D.C.: Potomac Books.

Potter, John Deane. 1967. *Yamamoto: The Man Who Menaced America*. New York: Paperback Library.

Prange, Gordon W. 1981. *At Dawn We Slept: The Untold Story of Pearl Harbor*. New York: McGraw Hill.

Ransom, Roger L. 1968. "British Policy and Colonial Growth: Some Implications of the Burden from the Navigation Acts." *Journal of Economic History* 28 (September 1968): 427–435.

Ransom, Roger L., and Richard Sutch. 1988. Capitalists Without Capital: The Burden of Slavery and the Impact of Emancipation. *Agricultural History* 62 (Fall): 119–147.

Ransom, Roger L., and Richard Sutch. 2001. Conflicting Visions: The American Civil War as a Revolutionary Conflict. *Research in Economic History* 20: 249–301.

Ransom, Roger. 2018. *Gambling on War: Confidence, Fear and the Tragedy of the First World War.* London: Cambridge University Press.

Service, Robert. *Stalin: A Biography.* Cambridge, MA: Belknap Press of Harvard University Press, 2006.

Singer, J. David., and Melvin Small. 1972. *The Wages of War, 1816–1965: A statistical Handbook.* New York: John Wiley and Sons.

Taylor, Alan. 2016. *American Revolutions: A Continental History, 1750–1804.* New York: W.W. Norton.

The Formation of the First German Nation-State, 1800–1871 1993

Thomas, Evan. 2006. *Sea of Thunder: Four Commanders and the Last Great Naval Campaign, 1941–45.* New York: Simon and Schuster.

Thomas, Hugh. 2005. *Rivers of Gold: The Rise of the Spanish Empire From Columbus to Magelloan.* New York: Random House.

Tyler, Sydney. 1905. *The Japan-Russia War: An Illustsrated History of the War in the Far East, The Greatest Conflict of Modern Times.* kindle ed. Philadelphia.

Walton, Timothy. 1994. *The Spanish Treasure Fleets.* New Yori.

Winders, Richard Bruce. 2002. *Crisis in the Southwest: The United States, Mexico, and the Struggle over Texas.* New York: SR Books.

Wolf, Nikolaus. 2013. Europe's Great Depression: Coordination Failure after the First World War. In *The Great Depression of the 1930s*, ed. Nicholas Crafts and Peter Fearon, 74–109. Oxford, UK: Oxford University Press.

GPSR Compliance

The European Union's (EU) General Product Safety Regulation (GPSR) is a set of rules that requires consumer products to be safe and our obligations to ensure this.

If you have any concerns about our products, you can contact us on

ProductSafety@springernature.com

In case Publisher is established outside the EU, the EU authorized representative is:

Springer Nature Customer Service Center GmbH
Europaplatz 3
69115 Heidelberg, Germany